# Doggedly

# Doggedly

Musings on the Breeding, Judging and Preservation of Purebred Dogs

**DENISE FLAIM**

REVODANA PUBLISHING

81 Lafayette Avenue, Sea Cliff, N.Y. 11579

Copyright © 2020 Revodana Publishing

All rights reserved

ISBN: 978-1-943824-47-2

Without limiting the rights under copyright reserved above, no part of this publication may be reproduced, stored in or introduced into a retrieval system, or transmitted, in any form or by any means (electronic, mechanical, photocopying, recording or otherwise), without the prior written permission of the publisher.

The scanning, uploading and distribution of this book via the Internet or via any other means without the permission of the publisher is illegal.

www.revodanapublishing.com

Per Patrizio Palliani, un vero "dog man," con molto affetto e rispetto

"Everything which best fulfills a purpose is also beautiful."

— Friederun von Miriam-Stockmann, vom Dom Boxers

Front and back cover photos by Anna Szabó

# Table of Contents

Foreword .................................................................. 15
Introduction ............................................................. 19
Back to the Garden .................................................. 23
Let's Dish ................................................................. 31
Do Wrongs Ever Make a Right? ................................ 37
Seduce Me — Not .................................................... 47
Blunt Talk ................................................................. 53
House Proud ............................................................ 61
Word Play ................................................................. 67
Feast or Famine ....................................................... 73
How to Become a Sighthound Judge ....................... 81
Tough Question ........................................................ 91
Forgotten Voices ...................................................... 97
The Flutter of Familiarity ........................................ 105
In Defense of Beauty .............................................. 111
Present Company ................................................... 117
Getting Critical ....................................................... 123
What's in Your Genes? ........................................... 131
That's a Shame ....................................................... 139
Maid to Order ......................................................... 145
We Are Family ........................................................ 151
Of Highboys and Lowchen ..................................... 159
Tight Spots ............................................................. 165
What's in a Name? ................................................. 175
A Dog-Show Fairy Tale .......................................... 181
Mounting Concern .................................................. 187

Weimaraner

# Foreword

It is a privilege to be asked to be associated with this remarkable new book, an exceptional work by an exceptional writer.

Denise Flaim breeds Rhodesian Ridgebacks, but is a lover of dogs — all dogs. Her willingness to put her thoughts in writing for the world to see along with her command of language gives a richness to her subjects that we seldom experience. Her questions spark a deep, much-needed challenge to our perspectives on the breeds we love and cherish.

Too often people are involved with the breeding of dogs without the knowledge and research necessary to realize the dangers that lurk from a hereditary standpoint. Denise goes above and beyond with both her homework and her years of research when it comes to everything "dog." Because of her insatiable interest in learning, she also finds many additional subjects that run parallel

— or not so parallel — to ours. All of this makes her a very unique person in our dog world. The desire for knowledge is a wondrous thing, and those who have it and put their learning in print make us all better "dog people."

When it comes to "type" — the combination of characteristics that define a breed — I find that the majority of breeders and exhibitors think it refers only to heads, but it is *so* much more. Denise has such deep insight into dogs and their history that I hope her writings will open some conversation on the intricacies of "type," a word that we throw around so haphazardly. The value of any book is in the ability of the reader to use its information.

The essays about backcrossing and epigenetics are subjects to which we all need to give much more consideration. We are all set in our ways, and we all think, "Why change things if that is how we have always done it?" But maybe it is time to learn to think outside the box before it becomes necessary for us to do so.

One of my favorite books is *Blink* by Malcolm Gradwell, which is not about dogs at all, but it totally applies. If we trust our instincts, we are usually on the right path. Think, study, research and remember: "Unless you know the road you've come from, you cannot know where you are going." That old African proverb applies to every aspect of our sport.

*Doggedly* is a book for anyone who breeds, shows and/or judges purebred dogs. But it is also a treasure for anyone who appreciates good writing. Reading this book was a stimulating experience for me, and I hope it creates the same kind of awe for you.

**Pat Hastings**

*Judge, writer, lecturer and recipient of AKC's Lifetime Achievement Award*

Belgian Malinois

Author and French Bulldog

# Introduction

When I was an editor and columnist at the daily Long Island newspaper *Newsday* — remember newspapers? — one of the reporters had a sign above his desk.

"Just because I'm not typing," it read, "doesn't mean I'm not writing."

That sign was a clever way to rebuff snooping editors. But it was also a completely accurate statement of fact. When you are a writer, you never stop observing, thinking, asking, comparing, questioning — it's how you nod asleep at night, and how you awaken in the morning. And when you're a dog person — whether a breeder, dog-show exhibitor, judge or owner — you too are perennially expanding your knowledge of those impossibly endearing but maddeningly complex four-leggers, oftentimes finding the greatest illumination in the most unexpected places.

This book — a collection of essays that I have written over the years in the premier American dog magazine *Dog News* — does just that, wandering from the whelping box to the show ring, and everywhere in between, all the while celebrating the unlikely crevices and corners where our dog knowledge is expanded, and our connections deepened.

For those on the outside looking in, whose only experience with purebred dogs is the annual Westminster telecast, it's perhaps understandable that our world looks to be about hair-sprayed coifs and blue-blooded pedigrees. But we know better. Purebred dogs are a manifestation of every facet of our humanity — our quest for survival, the contours of our work ethic, the depths of our aesthetic, the vibrancy of our cultural values and the unassailability of our taboos. That, and not the garish flash of a blue ribbon, is what ties us so closely to the breeds we have come to call our own.

Writers and dog fanciers share another predilection, and that is an insatiable craving for perfection.

On a quixiotic quest to find just the right words, the writer is always constantly revising and revisiting her text, looking to give it clarity, depth and, yes, beauty. Similarly, breeding is also an act of self-expression, the breeder endlessly scrutinizing pedigrees and orchestrating pairings in the hopes of producing the next Great One. Though one is sitting at a keyboard, the other over a whelping box, both are trying to refine their vision, their interpretation, and the end result is uniquely their own.

Sadly, however, whether we are holding a pen or a lead, inevitably we fall short, because just as all prose has its shortcomings, so do all dogs. And in the end, that's as it should be, because what's the point in having nothing to strive for? As Sisyphus of Greek mythology taught us, it isn't the achievement that is so satisfying, but rather the full-throated pursuit of it.

## INTRODUCTION

The essays collected in this book are a celebration of that painstaking roll of the boulder up an eternally confounding mountain, and an affirmation of our failures as much as our successes as our efforts succumb to gravity and glide back down to ground zero yet again.

I hope you enjoy reading the pieces I've corralled in *Doggedly* as much as I enjoyed writing them over the years. Some take us backward, to the great dog men and women on whose shoulders we stand today. Others peer cautiously ahead, trying to divine the future of our beleaguered dog world, so much of it steeped in the traditions and sensibilities of long-departed centuries.

All, however, leave us right where we want to be — very much in the here and now, flanked by the dogs who represent the unbroken chain connecting us to who we have been, and who we are becoming.

My deepest thanks to *Dog News* publishers Matthew Stander and Gene Zaphiris for providing a place in their award-winning magazine for my writing, and for their friendship and support.

**Denise Flaim**

*Sea Cliff, New York*

Golden Retriever

# Back to the Garden

*Close encounters of the breeding kind.*

The last time I really tended my garden was almost a decade ago. My thumb had never been greener, and our house was scheduled to be on the village garden tour that spring.

On the appointed day, sunny and bright, the petal pushers arrived. They ogled my chaste tree, chucked my peonies under their frilly chins, admired the high-wire act of my Clematis montana. In the side yard, an eagle-eyed rosarian noted that I had mislabeled the Bourbon rose Louise Odier, then turned to my candy-cane-striped Variegata di Bologna and said encouragingly, "You should enter a rose show."

"You mean a show with ribbons and judges and placements?" I asked, my eyebrows lifted almost as high as the crape-myrtle branches overhead.

"Yes!" she responded brightly, sensing the possibility of a convert.

"Yeah — no," I answered, a bit too curtly. "I get more than enough of that from dog shows." And I beat a hasty retreat from the cognoscenti, back to the nice lady from Staten Island who couldn't tell a dahlia from a begonia.

Oh, the heights from which I've fallen. Soon after, the demands of children, home, work and, of course, dogs elbowed aside any extra time I had for my small but intensely planted Victorian garden. In the fall I stopped replenishing my tulip bulbs. In winter I tossed the nursery and seed catalogs. In spring I didn't give the roses their ritual wake-up cocktail of Epsom salts and compost. In summer I was too busy to unholster my Felco pruners, leaving my flower beds as unkempt as an Afghan Hound that hasn't been groomed in months.

This year, though, was different. This year I went back to the garden. And what I've found there, much to my surprise, is a parallel — and maybe a parable — about gardens and dogs.

Gardens, of course, are living metaphors. In their cycles and their seasons, their challenges and their triumphs, they resonate with almost every human activity. Including, it turns out, the breeding of purebred dogs.

Gardens ask us to make value judgments at almost every turn, just as our whelping boxes do. What makes one plant more desirable than another? What new addition is worthy of being planted here? How many weeds will I tolerate? Is the big picture more important than those few inevitable blemishes?

Gardens teach us the same lessons that dog breeding does. There's the necessity of

**Mastiff puppy.** Courtesy Yessica Sam-Sin.

patience: It has taken twenty years for my climbing hydrangea to live up to the first part of its name, and it can take what seems like an eternity for a line of dogs to truly establish itself. There's the importance of the long view: Most of the time, our endeavors in the garden and the whelping box are works in progress, showing only the fragments and not the whole, and we must be sustained by our vision of how things will ultimately turn out. And of course, we can't ignore the ephemeralness of it all: Though all gardens have a history and a progression, their successes are but a flashpoint in time, and then nature sweeps back in and demands to arm-wrestle for the next generation, Best in Show winner or not. You are never finished.

When a garden is left untended, the common plants — which, not coincidentally, are usually the hardiest — eventually engulf it. Last week I battled with a wild rose that had taken up residence beside the picket fence and grew a taproot that was wending its way down to Guangdong Province. It was certainly vigorous, throwing off octopus-like canes, but do its entirely unremarkable white blooms compare in any way to, say, my beloved climbing Angel Face floribunda, with its frilled, deep-lavender flowers and intense fragrance, redolent of citrus? As we progress in dogs, we too learn to appreciate the extraordinary. And we realize that before we know enough to pass over the mediocre — the endless cell-packs of impatiens at Home Depot — we must first learn to identity quality.

That said, Angel Face gave up the ghost in my garden long ago. It wanted a warmer spot, and was a magnet for black spot. How much coddling am I willing to give a plant, no matter how beautiful, in order to ensure its survival? It's a question we ask about our breeds, too. When do we get too fanciful? When does form overtake function, and is that ever acceptable? Do I want a breed that has become a hothouse flower, unable to survive without intense intervention? Where is the tipping point? For every gardener, and for every breeder, I suppose the answer is different.

Whether you're working with plants or dogs, you can't have it all, no matter what the feminist mantras say. When push comes to shove, you have to set your priorities. I grow old garden roses because I want a rose that looks like a puffy wad of tissue, with a smell that intoxicates and a general hardiness that will survive my pesticide-free precincts. To get that, I'm willing to live with one-time bloomers, and I avoid the more modern hybrid teas, which unfurl all summer, but have forgone some of their hardiness and scent in the bargain. It's the same with the dogs: We decide what our deal-breakers are, and we compromise on the rest.

Then there are the stealth plants, the ones that are beautiful and hardy and serve a definite purpose, but whose nature is to engulf every cubic square of earth in their vicinity. Bishop's weed, purple loosestrife, English ivy, trumpet vine — I debated bringing them all into the garden, asking if what they contributed would outweigh the inevitable difficulties I'd have keeping them at bay. They remind of the nagging faults — gay tails, overbites, high hocks — that can settle into a breeding program. "Do I want to breed to him and risk getting X, Y or Z?" we ask ourselves, knowing a stud dog's track record. And though we might yank them out of our breeding programs, and think we have them vanquished, they re-seed surreptitiously, and come back to surprise us another day.

Despite its modest size, this garden of mine is a lot of work. Still, I can't imagine hiring a landscaper. Not because I enjoy the kneeling and yanking and digging, but because, honestly, I can't be sure that the leaf-blower brigade knows what they're looking at. "Redbud? What's a redbud?" a landscaper asked me once, as I pointed to the native tree with the beautiful heart-shaped leaves in a nearby bed. Sadly, in dogs, I think we suffer from the same lack of not even connoisseurship, but just basic knowledge.

And, let's be honest: We like the feel of our hands in the soil. Which is why even the most accomplished breeders after a half-century or more often can't bear to disassemble their whelping boxes. When I first started in my breed, I traveled with my first bitch to the stud dog of a respected, long-tenured breeder whose kennel name is recognized internationally. She had a litter on the ground, which she said was her last. "I am like the old pear tree," she told me gravely. "And in its last seasons, it gives its best fruit." She was right about the pear tree — often the best blooms need old wood, and it is our longest-standing breeders who consistently produce the best dogs. But, thankfully, she was wrong about that being her last litter. The soil called her back.

At a dog show in Virginia recently, a friend admitted that she travels around with a shovel in her car, in case she comes across the site of an old homestead — the farm long gone, but the footprint of

**Siberian Husky**

a garden remaining. There is usually a stand of old irises, and she digs up the tubers and gives them a new home. Rose rustlers do this, too, hunting for antique roses in old cemeteries. When they take a clipping, they doubtless feel as exhilarated as we do when we happen across a dog with an old and precious pedigree, lines we thought forever lost and irreplaceable.

Like the plants we love, in all their variety and splendor, the dogs we cultivate are our efforts to keep nature controlled and coerced, however imperfectly. People will always garden, just as they will always breed. Attempting to bend nature to our will, to tame it, to stretch its boundaries, is just human nature. And nature pushes back with her capriciousness and, often, her cruelty. The magnolia blossoms that are decimated by an unexpected frost, the healthy litter felled by parvovirus — these are the unexpected heartbreaks that test your mettle.

My garden is mostly under control again now, after daily morning forays where I can lose myself for hours, much like studying pedigrees. I have lost a bit of ground by not tending things as meticulously as I would have liked this past decade, but it won't take much time to recover. That's the thing about having good bones — hardscapes, arbors, mature specimen trees — in your garden, or your dogs, for that matter: As long as you have a sound foundation, it's relatively easy to add the cosmetics.

And adding them I am. I've been on a bit of a clematis binge, and have worked up a list of roses I want to add when fall arrives. Angel Face is on there, perhaps despite my better judgment, but gardeners — and breeders — are gluttons for punishment, not to mention eternal optimists. But even if I get back to where I left off, I'll leave the rose shows to someone else. And if that makes me the horticultural equivalent of a backyard breeder — a backyard gardener, I guess — that's perfectly fine with me.

Yorkshire Terrier

# Let's Dish

*The difference between pottery and porcelain.*

There is a wonderful quote about purebred dogs attributed to the late Nigel Aubrey-Jones.

"Quality," wrote that great Pekingese breeder and judge, "is the difference between pottery and porcelain."

It is a superlative metaphor — if, that is, one knows a bit about the decorative arts. And in this paper-plate era in which we live, is there anyone left who can differentiate Meissen from Mikasa? We can only hope …

Let's dig a little bit, because, like all brilliant metaphors, this one works flawlessly on multiple levels.

Pottery goes by many names — earthenware, stoneware, terracotta, even "fine china." What they all have in common is their relative refinement — or lack thereof. Pottery clay is comprised of coarse grains, compared to porcelain, which has a much more distilled composition. Because of these rougher building blocks, pottery cannot be as fine as porcelain — the potter has to use broader strokes, if we can mix artistic metaphors.

It isn't much of a stretch to see how this corresponds to dogs. After all, God — or in this case, dog — is in the details. The finishing touches on a quality animal — the delicate veining on the muzzle of a Borzoi, the small, fine, rose ear of a Whippet, the silky, wildly exotic topknot of the Afghan Hound — can't be rendered precisely in a medium as crude as pottery. "Common" is the word used to describe a dog who is pottery — he has the overall appearance of the breed, but on closer examination he lacks the finer points that would elevate him above more than just average.

This also explains breed evolution, especially in newly established breeds, in which the "drag" of the breed — the undesirable qualities contributed by crosses or foundational contributors — crop up and impair type. In a way, this is akin to the larger clay particles found in pottery, which increase the likelihood of air bubbles that mar the finished piece. The more evolved and mature the breed, in theory the greater the likelihood that these rough patches have been eliminated or ground down, so they can mesh together and contribute to the end result instead of detracting from it.

Composition isn't the only difference between pottery and porcelain. There is another factor that is just as important, because it imparts the strength needed to temper the delicacy of porcelain. And that is heat.

Pottery is more affordable than porcelain not just because it is less detailed — and so takes less effort to sculpt — but also because it is fired at much lower temperatures, and for shorter periods of time. But the price to be paid for that is an object that is much softer, and so more prone to nicks, chips and general damage in everyday use. This is why a great big mixing bowl made of pottery is actually more likely to break than a small, finely modeled porcelain figurine.

Porcelain is harder and more durable than pottery because its smaller grains are fused together under much higher heat, and for a longer time. This gives porcelain its greater density, which is where its strength derives. And don't we notice that same quality, a solidity of muscle and fiber, in a quality dog, as if it has been carved out of marble? The very best dogs are born with this natural collectedness, rather than having it imposed on them through roadwork and other forms of intense conditioning.

But — giving literal meaning to the term "trial by fire" — the process of firing porcelain comes with attendant risks. The higher the temperature, the greater the strength of the finished object, but also the greater the risk that something will go awry. Cracking, crazing, bubbling, peeling, pinholes — any number of defects can mar a piece of porcelain if a step in the kiln process has been rushed or poorly thought out. And even the most meticulously planned firing can result in disaster because, as is the case with their breeding corollaries, the ceramics gods are infuriatingly capricious.

To bring us back to dogs again, it's obviously more difficult to produce a porcelain dog than a pottery one. The effort that goes into the former is much greater, and without good planning and a clear vision, the odds of something going very wrong are correspondingly higher. Then again, so are the potential rewards.

Finally, there is yet another defining difference between pottery and porcelain, and that is translucence, or an object's ability to allow light to pass through it. This is what gives a fine piece of porcelain its distinctive "glow." Pottery, by contrast, is flatly opaque.

When one sees a dog of great quality, there is a similar sense of illumination. What one sees radiating from such a dog is, essentially, true type. Like translucence, this is subtle, but obvious to the educated eye. All the time, effort, patience, discernment, quality material and aesthetics that go into a fine piece of porcelain — or a well-bred purebred dog — culminate in a final product that is to some degree transcendent.

And in the end, isn't that what true type is — glimpsing beyond the individual dog, to something greater? Not just blood and bone and muscle, but the cultures and civilizations, the human needs and aspirations, that gave rise to the creation of a breed? The bone-chilling tundra and gold-encrusted manor house of the Russian noble, the sand-swept dunes and fire-flickered tent of the Bedouin nomad, and everything in between?

Sadly, there are too many breeders and judges who don't understand that. And then there's the handful who do.

The difference between them, too, is that of pottery and porcelain.

LET'S DISH

**Whippets.** Courtesy AKC Museum of the Dog.

Xoloitzcuintli

# Do Wrongs Ever Make a Right?

*Sometimes, actually, they do.*

In a recent conversation, a long-time Hound breeder pondered why his breed is seeing so many catastrophic health issues of late, when decades ago such instances were the rare exception.

No one can say for sure, of course, but there are plenty of interesting theories. Perhaps it's Seek and Ye Shall Find syndrome: The more health problems we test for, the more we are likely to undercover — some of which have been there all along, blipping softly under the radar. Or it could be epigenetics, a fancy way of saying that ever-increasing toxins in our environment are "turning on" our dogs' genes, triggering autoimmune disease and more. Or you could argue for just the opposite, that our obsession with creating an antimicrobial world is actually weakening our dogs' immune systems, as we deprive them of the opportunity to mount normal responses to everyday pathogens.

Or maybe — and admittedly, we tread on "Freakonomics" territory here — we can blame it, as we do so much else in the decline of the dog world, on the American Kennel Club's decision in 2000 to require DNA testing of frequently used sires.

The "FUS" requirement has been reviled — in hindsight, of course — for opening the Pandora's box of declining litter and dog registrations. Commercial breeders bristled at the new restrictions and found, to their delight, that the American public's attention to acronyms was fuzzy at best. Most couldn't distinguish between papers from the AKC and any of the other lookalike registries, such as the APR (America's Pet Registry), NAPR (North American Purebred Registry) or DRA (Dog Registry of America, which was once the top result if you Googled "dog registry" or "dog papers"). So the AKC kissed a good portion of that revenue stream goodbye.

But perhaps another thing the mandatory DNA testing did, inadvertently of course, was to stem the genetic diversity that has been trickling into many breeds ever since the Victorians popularized the idea of closed registries and "purebred" dogs.

To be sure, we are flirting with sacrilege here, to suggest that purebred dogs are hardly pure. But none of our breeds sprang, Athena-like and fully formed, from the head of Zeus. Trace back far enough, and there was invariably some sort of canine cocktail, sometimes shaken, sometimes stirred, that brought their kind into being.

And the dirty secret of purebred dogs is that crossbreeding in various breeds was an occasional reality — and, some might argue, a necessity.

A textbook example of this is the Mastiff. A breed that has been pummeled by the

Ch. Ajax of Hellingley.

Ch. The Devil of Wayside.

vagaries of history, the Mastiff has seen, even required, the addition of other breeds, in particular after both world wars, when it was almost decimated in its native England. In many quarters, the occasional introduction of new blood was blithely tolerated, even encouraged. In his 1975 book *Take Them Round Please: The Art of Judging Dogs*, British judge Tom Horner includes a photo of the "splendidly sound" late-19th-Century Mastiff Ch. Ajax of Hellingly. "This dog's dam was served by two dogs in the same heat — a lucky accident, indeed!" Horner wrote. Presumably, they were both Mastiffs, but the philosophy is the same: Sometimes practicality wins out over paper.

Tolerance of such porous pedigrees in the 19th Century, when many breeds were still in an embryonic stage, is perhaps more understandable than today. But it occurred in the last century as well. In 1959, a purebred Dogue de Bordeaux bitch, Fidelle de Fénélon, was imported into the U.S., and was subsequently registered as a Mastiff by the American

Above left: **Heatherbelle Portia of Goring and some of her 12 puppies, 1950.** Above right: **Tobin Jackson and Ch. Deer Run Wycliff.** Photos courtesy Molosser Magazin.

Kennel Club. That's not apocryphal: It's right there in the studbook at the AKC library. Bred to a bona-fide Mastiff, Merles Alvin, Fidelle produced offspring that went on to produce specialty winners; one of her descendants, the well-known brindle, Devil of Wayside, was exported to Great Britain, where he became a champion and influential sire.

Perhaps the most famous allegations of cross-pollination in the breed were in the 1970s and '80s, in the Frenchtown, New Jersey, kennel of Tobin Jackson. Jackson's Deer Run line is omnipresent in Mastiff pedigrees today; knowledgeable fanciers put the number of DRF ("Deer Run Free") lines at less than one percent, worldwide. And that's probably too conservative a number. No one I have ever interviewed saw an actual breeding between a Great Dane or a Saint Bernard and a Mastiff, but many argue that the dogs themselves demonstrated it clear as day: First, from impressively headed but decidedly unsound British-based stock (the late handler Alan Levine likened them to circus seals crossing the ring), Deer Run produced very sound, but relatively plain dogs. Then, once the structural issues were sorted, the dogs regained type — along with longer coats (the infamous "fluffies") and the occasional piebald. Jackson isn't around to tell the tale, but at the end of the day he left the breed sounder and just as typey as he found it. Does it matter how he got there?

(Jackson was also a beachhead for the Presa Canario in the late 1980s and early '90s, and his Deer Run Arbaco was a foundation dog here in the U.S. Controversy about that dog rages even today, as Spanish Presa breeders argue that his blue pigment was unheard of in the county of origin, and point to the fact that Jackson had a diminutive Neapolitan Mastiff on premise. The debate over whether or not the AKC's first recorded Presa was in fact a mongrel has created a schism in the breed, with "purists" renaming it the Dogo Canario. Descendants of Jackson's Presas include Bane, who attacked and killed San Francisco lacrosse coach Diane Whipple in her apartment-building hallway in 2001.)

Mastiffs are hardly the only breed where incursions of foreign blood have happened with regularity. Sometimes, the crossing is intentional — a not-unknown happening, for example, in some of the closely related Terrier breeds. Other times, it's simply an oops. In my own breed, Rhodesian Ridgebacks, we sometimes see blue Ridgebacks, as well as black-and-tan anomalies. Some of my less cynical peers see these "off" colors as "throwbacks" to founding Rhodesian dogs at the turn of the previous century — blue Danes or Greyhounds and Airedales, is the common refrain. But I apply Occam's razor:

The simplest explanation is likely the best. Blue Ridgebacks are particularly common in Germany, native home of the Weimaraner. And the Doberman-Ridgeback cross was a very popular one in southern Africa, when an edgier guarding temperament was desired. Both phenotypes are close enough to Ridgeback type that even a first-generation cross could "pass" and continue on in the gene pool.

The operant question is not: Do these crosses happen? But rather: Is it a bad thing that they no longer do — or, at least, have less opportunity to, without being detected? Did these occasional crosses, made possible by a registry that operated on the honor system, help their respective breeds? Did the end justify the means?

Of course, the problem with such "paper hanging" is that it degrades the value of pedigrees, sometimes to the point of absurdity. Anyone who deals in Neapolitan Mastiffs from the country of origin will tell you that some pedigrees are as fictitious as a canto by Dante. When working with any of these bloodlines, a breeder needs access to a parallel universe of pedigrees — the real ones — known by a handful of knowledgeable breeders. Like Dante, without a Virgil to guide you, you're stuck in genetic purgatory.

Perhaps the reason that these crosses happen in secret is the reaction when they are done out in the open. Consider the Dalmatian Backcross Project: In 1973, one Pointer — *one* Pointer — was crossed to a Dalmatian to help eliminate a uric-acid stone problem that had become endemic in the breed. To say this ignited a huge debate in the Dalmatian community would be an understatement. The offspring of this cross — themselves bred back to purebred Dalmatians for four decades — were barred from registration until 2011, when the AKC permitted their inclusion in the registry, albeit with a notation of their spotty — or, in this case, not-so-spotty — history.

A sharp contrast to this is the story of the bobtail Boxers bred in the United Kingdom, in anticipation of the ban on tail docking. Bruce Cattanach, a successful Boxer breeder, crossed Boxers with Pembroke Welsh Corgis that had a naturally occurring bobtail gene. As you might imagine, the first generation of this cross was a Puggle-like creature that had little resemblance to a Boxer. But with subsequent breedings back to the Boxer side of the pedigree, the dogs soon regained type — all the while naturally losing their tails, thanks to the Corgi DNA that was being pulled along. After four generations of purebred breedings, the Kennel Club permits backcrossed offspring to be registered as purebred, as these Corgi-derived creatures were. The earth continued to spin on its axis.

I recently corresponded with a Scottish Deerhound breeder in the United Kingdom who crossed to a Greyhound to bring some genetic diversity to the breed. She has much more work ahead of her, of course, but under the British system there is a light at the end of the tunnel: After breeding back to purebred Deerhounds after the required number of generations, her dogs will be considered purebred — and registerable.

There is, of course, a very good reason why purebred breeders balk at the idea of diluting their gene pools with other breeds, however wise the cross might be, and that is, quite simply, the risk of unwanted qualities surfacing later along with the wanted ones. It is already dauntingly difficult to breed typey, sound and well-temperamented dogs from a closed gene pool; when a torrent of new DNA roils the waters, getting back on course can be frighteningly difficult.

For a cautionary tale, consider yet-another Molosser example: Knowledgeable and tenured Cane Corso breeders (a rare breed in their own right) will tell you that their breed's "restoration" — the period when they were permitted to cross to other breeds to widen the breeding pool — has left them with endless headaches in the whelping box. And judges are seeing it in the show ring (though, alarmingly, some may not know it) in dogs whose lack of bone and bug-eyed expression echo the Boxer blood not so very far behind them, or whose rounded skulls give evidence of more recent Bullmastiff infusions. As a result of all this backcrossing — not to mention the fact that the best tool for overriding this drag and re-establishing type, linebreeding, has fallen out of favor worldwide — the Cane Corso is teetering on the precipice, so overwhelmed by outside genetic influences that breed type is slipping away.

It's a delicate job to balance breed stability on the one hand and genetic diversity on the other, and for many decades, a kind of "Don't ask, don't tell policy" prevailed. The hurdles were so high, the stigma so deep, that only mavericks (some would choose another noun) dared break the rules. Because if they did, they had to falsify pedigrees to keep their dogs in the breeding pool.

Today, with pedigrees that can be policed with all the genetic forensics of a "Law and Order" episode, even being unethical is an increasingly distant option. Deprived of this trickle of new genetic material, are our gene pools growing stagnant? Is it time for a mechanism to permit the very occasional case of limited, controlled and intelligent crossbreeding — where it can be demonstrably warranted — to improve health and type? It should go without saying — but let's say it anyway — that such allowances would have to be balanced by necessary and conservative safeguards, including a special prefix or code on the pedigrees of these crossbred offspring, so that breeders who wish to avoid them in their lines could identify them at a glance.

We could start, perhaps, with a campaign to teach our breeders the basics of canine genetics. It is frightening — and not a little embarrassing — to consider how many breeders out there have not the foggiest idea. Breeding may be an art, but before you go all Picasso on your breed, you should have a minimal understanding of the very real genetic theories underscoring it. Recently, going through old papers at my parents' home,

I came across a multiple-choice test I took in seventh grade that had questions about simple recessive inheritance and Gregor Mendel. (I took a long, hopeful sniff, but, alas, the purple ink had long ago relinquished that weirdly intoxicating mimeograph smell.) Anyway, the point: *Seventh* grade. Is it too much to ask that our breeders have a command of the science commensurate with a middle-schooler?

Similarly, in many breeds we are not doing enough to educate breeders about correct breed type. If they don't know what it is, how can they hope to preserve it? Through misguided pairings and equally misguided selection, they do more damage to their breed than any crossbreeding could.

The thing we love most about dogs is their mutability. They have the genetic elasticity of Gumby. A breed can be decimated, and then reconstructed, as long as there are clever and masterful breeders at the helm. (Case in point: the Irish Wolfhound, which was essentially re-created with Scottish Deerhound and Great Dane blood, with possibly a Tibetan Mastiff thrown in for good measure.) A dog so tightly linebred it ought to have three heads can, in just one breeding, produce offspring with a coefficient of inbreeding of zero. A dog, a line, a breed is never fixed and constant, at least never for long. Not to be too Buddhist about it, but dogs are a continuum, an expanse, a work in progress. Rather than being a threat, that ought to be a source of encouragement.

What's the right answer? If anything were that clear cut, the title of this essay wouldn't have culminated in a question mark. But what's unambiguous is this: We need to start having the conversation. In an age when longstanding cultural taboos in our own society are being undone at a dizzying pace, we need to take a fresh, clear-eyed look at our own canine ones. In the end, people may not agree, and that's perfectly fine. But what isn't fine is that they should be made to feel they are committing treason or sacrilege for broaching the conversation in the first place.

Chihuahua

# Seduce Me — Not

*Who wouldn't like to be swept off their feet?*

Forget that steamy après-show rendezvous at the Red Roof. The seductions I'm talking about happen fully clothed, in plain sight, right in the middle of the ring.

Every culture has its aesthetics, from the facial tattoos of the Maori to the super-stretched earlobes of the Masai. Beauty is very much in the eye of the beholder, and those beholders derive their ideas from the culture percolating around them.

In today's dog-show world, beauty is often interpreted as fluid, smooth, undulating lines and ground-covering movement, with ample — some would say excessive — reach and drive, head carried up like a periscope, eyes well above the topline. This is our Brigitte Bardot, the desirable outline that makes us stop and gawk, like construction workers on a midtown lunch break.

But for some breeds, that ideal is utterly wrong. A Dogue de Bordeaux who moves with his head up is decidedly atypical, as basic physics would suggest: A pear-shaped body that bears an inordinate amount of weight on its front assembly logically must lower its head as its speed increases. Yet every year at that big Madison Square Garden show, I watch as beautiful examples of the breed have their necks yanked mercilessly every few steps by an assortment of otherwise competent professionals. But the owner-handlers, channeling their inner Raymond Triquets, know better.

(If you don't know Raymond Triquet, you have seen his invisible hand in dozens of FCI breed standards, as he has chaired that committee for many years. The literal savior of the Dogue de Bordeaux and author of its standard, he is one of the few breed prophets honored in his own land, as Dogue fanciers hang on his every word, and rightly so. His aptly named *Saga of the Dogue de Bordeaux* is required reading.)

Even in those breeds where a stereotypical silhouette and movement are desirable, there can be too much of a good thing. Sometimes it takes an outsider to point this out — that old all-rounder-versus-breeder-judge nugget.

Back to the topic of seduction. While today that word has an unavoidably sexual undercurrent, its original 16$^{th}$-Century meaning was more a political one, such as persuading a vassal to desert his allegiance. As breeders and judges, haven't we similarly pledged ourselves to the standard of each breed? And if that standard describes a particular outline or gait or presentation, who are we to lay down our arms and follow another aesthetic that is more familiar?

"The resistance of a woman to a man's advances is not always a sign of virtue," opined 17th-Century Frenchwoman Ninon de Lenclos on the subject of seduction. "Sometimes it's just a sign of experience."

Though she was a courtesan, de Lenclos knew something about romantic restraint: After reduced family circumstances drove her into prostitution, she was determined to be financially independent, and in the end chose men on her own terms. "Ninon always had crowds of adorers but never more than one lover at a time, and when she tired of the present occupier, she said so frankly and took another," wrote the Duke of Saint-Simon. "Yet such was the authority of this wanton, that no man dared fall out with his successful rival; he was only too happy to be allowed to visit as a familiar friend."

Sounds like the definition of sportsmanship.

As Madam de Lenclos rightly pointed out, to be seduced implies an abandonment of your own priorities in the face of someone else's. And isn't that what happens in the ring when a judge points at an exhibit with a head-turning trait that is being "sold" by the handler so that it eclipses the dog's shortcomings, no matter how serious? A gorgeously arched neck, for example, can seduce a judge into pointing, even when accompanied by stubby legs on a supposed-to-be-greyhound-like Irish Wolfhound, or exposed haws on a needs-to-be-tight-skinned Leonberger.

But while it is easy to blame the canine Casanova, there is complicity on the part of the judge, too.

"Seduction isn't making someone do what they don't want to do," wrote the journalist Benjamin Russell. "Seduction is enticing someone into doing what they secretly want to do already."

Kerry Blue Terrier

Let's admit it: Who doesn't admire a beautifully presented animal, trained and trimmed to perfection? Who doesn't appreciate a melting expression, or a stunningly crested neck, or the drama of handler and dog flying around the ring, legs pumping and hair flying?

It's one thing to recognize these come-hither elements, but an altogether different thing to act on them ... Shades of "I can just look, can't I?"

At the risk of getting hopelessly entangled in this rather risqué metaphor (and I'll bet there will be at least one reader who entirely misses the analogy and interprets this as a call for conjugality — sigh), seduction in the ring is in every sense a fling — electrifying in the moment but often supremely unsatisfying in hindsight, as such decisions are always predicated on lack of familiarity.

Much less exciting, but ultimately more rewarding, is a relationship with a breed standard based on fidelity. Old fashioned, I know. But true love requires knowledge, choosing the object of your attention after fully seeing and accepting both virtues and flaws — as opposed to, say, a come-hither selfie, artfully crafted with flattering angles and fuzzy filters. How does that illusion reconcile with the sun-drenched realities of the morning after? Yep, grab your car keys and flee.

So even if you flirt with the idea of a dalliance in the ring, in the end, point to the dog you'd want to take home to Mother.

Lady Anne Blunt

# Blunt Talk

*In search of 'aseel'*

I spent my weekend wandering the desert with an Englishwoman who's been dead for 101 years. You?

The century-long departed is Lady Anne Blunt — 15th Baroness of Wentworth, daughter of famous female mathematician Ada Lovelace, granddaughter of the poet Lord Byron, and eponymous owner of the Lady Blunt Stradivarius, the famous violin that sold earlier this decade for nearly $16 million.

Her impressive pedigree aside, my interest in Lady Blunt is in her legacy as a horse breeder. With her husband, the poet Wilfrid Scawen Blunt, this enterprising Victorian traveled exhaustively through the Middle East, pitching tents in desert hollows, subsisting on fried locusts and clove-spiked coffee, and negotiating with gift-obsessed Bedouins to acquire pure stock for her Crabbet Arabian Stud. Today, more than a century later, most purebred Arabian horses the world over have at least one Crabbet ancestor in their pedigrees.

Lady Blunt wrote two books about her travels, but both were heavily edited by her husband, whose chronic — and often overlapping — dalliances eroded their marriage and led to legal wrangling over the Crabbet empire. By contrast, in Lady Blunt's published journals, which document her travels from 1878 to 1917, her restrained but incisive voice comes through, revealing a savvy buyer whose eye for a horse could teach judges of any species a thing or two. (Lady Blunt is still well known among Arabian-horse enthusiasts. Can we say the same in the dog fancy for names like Sunny Shay, or Alva Rosenberg, or Hayes Blake Hoyt?) And as the great judge and Elkhound breeder Pat Trotter has shown from her study of the writings of Italian thoroughbred breeder Federico Tesio, successful horse people have much to impart about our parallel efforts in dogs.

Punctuating Blunt's writings is the word *asil* (also spelled *aseel*), an Arabic term meaning "pure," "noble" or "authentic," with the implication of many generations of pure breeding. Bedouins obviously did not maintain extensive written records of their livestock, so Blunt became a quick study of the oral history of the various desert lines. Her assessment of pedigree was based on phenotype only, as eager sellers could, and often did, invent provenances that were as enticing as they were fictitious.

(Lady Blunt acquired desert dogs, too, referring to them as "greyhound" and "slouguy," though Saluki experts claim them as their own.)

Back to the horses: "We saw a great number of mares ... but of the whole stud I saw only one mare I really cared for," Blunt wrote from Baghdad in February of 1878. "She is black, or nearly black, must be nearly 15 hands, fine shoulder and head and neck, and good hindquarters and short bones below the knee and hock and general appearance of being thoroughbred. On asking her breed I was told Kehailan Ajuz — and can believe it."

Lady Blunt's critique of the black mare illustrates her priorities: Size was important; a good forehand and rear, critical. She noted when a horse's conformation appeared built for speed, though she also commented on shallow thoraxes, which would impede endurance.

Less tangible but just as important was the air of noble breeding that stamped an Arabian as *asil* — going back to the black mare, that "general appearance of being thoroughbred." Lady Blunt often assessed people in this manner as well, basing the assumption of good breeding on the quality of a person's teeth or a calm comportment.

The opposite of *asil* is *kadish*, a horse without pedigree usually considered too common to ride, and so was used for drafting or other heavy work.

"She lumbers about like a carthorse, and as Mohammed got a fall off her, we saw her at great advantage for she got loose," Blunt wrote about a four-year-old brought for her to inspect, which she dismissed as a "regular *kadish*." "She galloped about like a cow and disgusted us beyond anything."

In his Daughter of the Wind blog, Arabian-horse enthusiast and breeder Edouard al-Dahdah explains that he heard the word *kadish* during his childhood in the Middle East, used dismissively to describe "common horses" that have "no origins."

"Clearly there was no pride of ownership of a *kadish*, as in Arabians," he writes, explaining that the word comes from the Arabic *qatasha*, meaning to sever or cut. "It seemed like these horses had fallen off some Garden of Eden of horses, and that nobody wanted to reminisce about that fall."

**Ghazu in the Wady Sirhan.** From "A Pilgrimage to Nejd, Vol. 1," by Lady Anne Blunt, 1881.

In his blog, al-Dahdah tells two stories about how cultural values differ over how quickly an *asil* animal can become *kadish*. In the first, a group of *asil* horses from a famous Bedouin clan in the 1970s were sold to Saudi Arabia. A bureaucratic snafu delayed the deal for so long that the original owners died or moved, and the horses were sold as *kadish*, "yet they are the same horses which were treasured by their Bedouin owners a few years earlier, and coveted by Saudi buyers," al-Dahdah muses.

In the other example, the Duke of Veragua — the last direct descendent of Christopher Columbus — lost his life and stud records during the Spanish Civil War of the 1930s. His stable of undocumented but purebred Arabians (many from Lady Blunt's Crabbet line) were incorporated into the Spanish government's breeding program. "These Veragua horses, in a Bedouin setting, would have automatically lost their purebred status, and would have been considered *kadish*," al-Dahdah notes. Western standards, however, were far more forgiving.

Returning to our black mare, Lady Blunt identified her breed as Kehailan Ajuz, which we can deconstruct: The first word, Kehailan, was her strain (in Arabic, *rasan*, which means "rope"), a reference to her maternal bloodline. The second word, Ajuz, was her substrain, which in Arabic was called *marbat* — literally, "the place where the rope is tied." The *marbat* was usually the person associated with that strain, which makes the Arabic metaphor so lovely, if we imagine a breeder to be the post to which a breed is tethered.

As the previous *kadish* stories illustrate, so close was this connection between breeders and their animals that if the transfer of stock to a new breeder was not deliberate, the line lost its purebred status — the rope, in essence, frayed.

We see a version of this two-tiered breeding identity in our own Western kennels. Think about any master breeder who leaves a kennel to a hand-picked successor: The kennel name endures, but with the change of *marbat*, the dogs soon change, too, even with the best intentions to stay the original course. The ensuing stock may be just as good (though usually not), but even so, it will be different, because choosing breeding animals and in turn selecting from their offspring is as individual as a fingerprint.

Crabbet Farm itself is a case in point. Lady Blunt's evolution as she crossed the desert is fascinating to witness: She started each day with coffee and camel's milk, brandished a pistol when a rival tribe swooped in for a *ghazu*, or raid, and visited harems and sheik tents alike. Similarly, she chose horses based on the teachings of her mentors, including Ottoman Turk Ali Pasha Sherif, who impressed on her the importance of tractability, soundness, speed and athleticism. The desert-bred Arabian, perfected for endurance, speed and warfare in one of the harshest climates on earth, "needs no improvement," Lady Blunt concluded.

After Lady Blunt's death, her daughter Judith took over the Crabbet stud. The new Lady Wentworth did not go to the desert for new blood, but rather looked to Poland, Russia and other countries that had established Arabian breeding programs. Lady Judith preferred horses with neotenic, or juvenile features, including deeply dished faces, foreshortened muzzles, wide foreheads and large, expressive eyes. Today, modern Arabians with that exaggerated, "seahorse-style" head have overtaken the breed, and are criticized as much as some of our usual-suspect dog breeds that find themselves in the animal-rights crosshairs.

When does a breed start to wander irredeemably into hypertype — that 50-cent word for "too much of a good thing"? Hard to tell, and perhaps to find that answer, we need to rejoin Lady Blunt astride her desert-bred mare. Of course, thorny questions follow us there, too, including this one: What makes her 19th Century Arabians superior to ones from the many centuries that preceded them?

All we can know for sure is that breeds, like desert sands, ultimately shift and drift: Life is, after all, about evolution, and our dog breeds are no more and no less than our relationship with long-ago eras and cultures. We have to find ongoing meaning in those relationships, or we no longer have reason to sustain them.

But knowing how quickly the present tends to blanket over the past should make us that much more interested in the cultures that brought our individual breeds to life. In that respect, breed history becomes the canine equivalent of an oasis — often stubbornly elusive, but indispensible, if these fragile canine caravans that we call breeds are to survive the relentless march of time with any shred of authenticity.

Wilfred Scawen Blunt, Lady Anne Blunt and friends.

Pug

# House Proud

*A real-estate search prompts comparisons to dog judging.*

Buildings are made of brick and mortar, plaster and joists. Dogs are made of blood and bone, fur and an altogether different kind of nail.

The two couldn't be more different, especially when you consider the big picture, like … oh, I don't know … sentience. (Amityville Horror aside, that is.) But lately, as I scroll through Zillow and Trulia listings in search of an urban investment property, I've been thinking of how much dogs and real estate have in common.

I'm not the first to make the comparison. The late, great dog man Percy Roberts launched the now well-worn metaphor of the standard as the blueprint, the breeder as the builder, and the judge as the building inspector. I've often thought that comparing the judge to an architectural critic is a better fit, because dogs need to be more than just structurally sound and functional: If they aren't also beautiful and typey, then what's the point or pleasure in that?

The job of the judge, like the critic, is to find the most functional dog in the most pleasing package — equal parts science and art, left brain and right, form and function. After all, you don't appreciate the Louvre solely because it keeps the rain off the Mona Lisa.

As I embark on my house hunting, I have different criteria for an investment property as opposed to my personal residence — not unlike the differences between a brood bitch and a show dog.

The place where you live — and the dog that you promote — can be as much about emotion as practicality. The intricate carving in a baluster, the streams of sunlight that flood the breakfast nook, the stately willow in the backyard … those are as compelling a reason for choosing to live somewhere as are a new boiler or Andersen windows. It's important to most of us for our homes to mirror who we are — it's our banner to the outside world, a reflection of our tastes, social status, even political leanings.

Similarly, when we special a show dog, the only criteria we need to satisfy is our own. How many top-winning dogs have you known that in ways large and small have defied their breed standards? The reasons for this can be many — perhaps the dog is a favored "heart dog," or perhaps the breeder has decided she "prefers" his googly-eyed expression or Edward Scissorhands grooming job to the more correct requirements set out in the standard. With the right handler, advertising and budget, such a dog can be successful in the relative eye blink of time that a specials campaign can last.

But there's no room for suspension of reality when you are talking about a rental property or a breeding animal. Both are investments, valuable not just for what they are in the moment, but for the untapped potential they represent. Their success depends on the long term. Some exist in relative anonymity, disconnected from your public life, but providing an invaluable resource for the future.

When you talk about such producers, curb appeal only goes so far, and here is where the fancy, dramatic show dogs fade away. Theoretically, we are supposed to evaluate breeding stock in the ring. There are some sins you can forgive, and others you cannot: No matter how beautiful, a Great Dane with the bone of a Greyhound is a pass. So is a sound Cane Corso who carries the parallel head planes of a Neapolitan. Pretty, but unpardonable, because the truly educated in those breeds will not — and should not — reward them. Similarly, as I tromp through house after house, there are some with flaws so fatal they cannot overcome their virtues, like the turn-key Queen Anne with the bedroom too small to fit a bed, or the charming townhouse with impossibly steep stairs.

Stretching the metaphor even further, consider house stagers and dog handlers: Talented ones can make a mediocre anything looks like a million bucks. The tens of thousands of house flippers weaned on HGTV have learned to bedazzle buyers with front doors painted a "statement" shade of cherry or canary, bamboo-laminate floors, exposed brick and stainless-steel appliances. Often, such foolers are intended to distract your eye from the flooded basement or crumbling stucco façade — not unlike how that talented handler keeps running his hand over his setter's beautifully crested neck, hoping you will ignore the wonky rear behind it.

No, what I want is the real-estate equivalent of an unpolished owner-handler — the guy with two left feet in "Best in Show." I want a house that is a diamond in the rough, like that mediocre handler whose ineptitude initially eclipses the once-in-a-lifetime dog on the leash beside him. Like an honest, well-maintained, details-spared townhouse with drop ceilings and faux wood paneling, I can see beyond it. And I have learned from experience that a lot of people can't.

In these as in all things, mentors are indispensible. In the house market where I am looking, I have a superb realtor whose prime imperative is to educate me before he sells to me. There is a complicated web of variables I need to learn, from the locations of mass transit lines to the nesting patterns of millennial renters. It's the true meaning of mentoring — that slow drip-drip-drip of information, absorbed through seeing and touching, with lots of room and time for questions, and still more questions. It's the only way to learn, whether you are talking about Victorians or Vizslas.

I also have a dear friend who lives in suburbia just outside the gritty city neighborhoods I am

Chow Chow

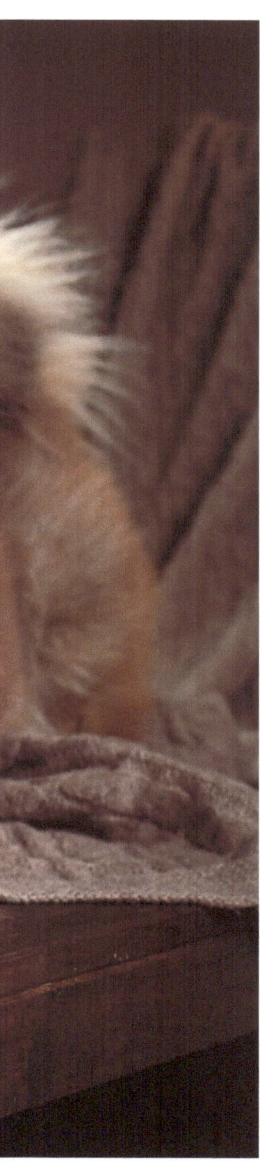

canvassing. If I give him the address of a house I just toured, he can tell me precisely what the history, architecture and tenor of the neighborhood are. I half-expect him to mention the empty soda can at the curb, so spot on is his analysis. But he grew up in these quarters, and he knows them on a level that is beyond verbal — he *feels* them. He's like a master breeder poring over pedigrees, pointing out the big-winning but terrible producers to avoid, and the quiet, uncelebrated dogs of quality who passed below most everyone else's radar.

In dogs as in everything, we crave authenticity, but we can't be shackled by the past: If you asked me to own Ridgebacks as they looked and behaved when their standard was first written in 1922, or even earlier, I should murmur a polite "no thank-you." Everything must accede to the age in which it now exists, and the trick comes with reconciling where the breed has been with where it is going.

So too is it with these gentrifying neighborhoods, their ghosts plainly evident in the ancient Italian ladies who sweep the fallen leaves in front of their immaculate row houses, and their futures telegraphed in the glinting nose rings of the hipsters who stroll through with their designer baby carriages and Frenchies on lead. The trick is in honoring the past while welcoming the future, whether you are in the show ring or on the city block. And always — always — being able to recognize true quality, which shines through in any age, flippers be damned.

English Foxhound

# Word Play

*JMO on breed standards, FWIW.*

Put down the smart phone and place your hands on the bookshelf, nice and easy, right where I can see them.

This shorthand age of emojis and acronyms is frustrating for language geeks like me. LOL all you like, but I see words as glittering rocks strewn about the landscape of a sentence, just begging to be brushed off, turned over, examined, contemplated. And nowhere is that truer than in our breed standards, most of which have withstood the test of time startlingly well. Even with its occasional obsolete phrase, the English Foxhound standard — which I'm told on good authority was drafted in a bar on the back of an envelope — is far better than most of us could do with a MacBook and some synonym-generating websites.

Yes, true wordsmiths — some poets, even — penned our standards. Think of the Fox Terrier's "on the tip-toe of expectation," the Mastiff's "grandeur and good nature," and of course the Afghan Hound's "eyes gazing into the distance as if in memory of ages past."

But the best standards are as precise as they are lyrical, and I don't mean in the sense of being so jargony that they are nearly impenetrable, like the opening line of the Dogue de Bordeaux's FCI standard: "Typical concave lined brachycephalic molossoid." If you need me, I'll be having a Hendrick's and tonic with those Foxhound fellas.

Mathematical ratios and anatomical terms aside, our breed standards are richly descriptive, and their words were not selected arbitrarily. I've often thought it would be interesting to take an adjective common to several standards, like "handsome" or "dignified," and see what conformational traits those breeds have in common. (Ironically, "pretty" — that ubiquitous compliment used ringside, as in "That's so pretty!" — is used in no standard I know of, but that's another discussion altogether.)

Adjectives in breed standards often have multiple levels of meaning. Consider, for example, eye shape. Breeds whose eyes should be large and round tend to be described as "friendly" and "gay" (in the 19th-Century sense, that is). Conversely, dogs with smaller, more oblique eyes are matched with descriptions such as "keen" and "fearless." This reflects their function: Dogs bred purely for companionship almost always have that open eye (which our reptilian brain registers as non-threatening), while those that guard have a smaller one — the eye of the predator, not the prey — because of the need to minimize exposure and injury from enemies.

Functionality aside, we also attribute personality traits to these physical qualities. Big, round eyes evoke the gentleness and innocence of babies or gentle prey animals (think "doe-eyed"), while slitted, small eyes are often associated with a certain toughness — in people as well as dogs.

For an interesting example of this anthropomorphizing in dog standards, consider "noble." That word landed on my radar screen when one of my mentors mentioned that the "noble" expression called for in the Bloodhound standard derives from the length and relative narrowness of the head.

That started me thinking about our human concepts of nobility. Tour a European castle, or the classical-art galleries of a museum, and over and over again you'll encounter the aquiline or Roman nose — like the Bloodhound's head, long and relatively lean, with an added curve. (When we think of parallels between human and canine conformation, what we call our nose is really the dog's muzzle, as we are taking about the entire nasal cavity — not just the button of pigmented flesh at its terminus.)

We underestimate it today, but throughout history the nose was believed to telegraph a person's social rank, power, even intelligence, likely derived from its close proximity to the brain. That's why ancient Greek and Roman statues are often missing their noses, which were chipped or chiseled off out of spite.

Many of history's most memorable figures — King David, Marc Anthony, Dante Alighieri, pick your favorite Egyptian Pharaoh — all had noses that were aquiline, derived from the Latin word for "eagle," which of course has a long, curved beak. So strong was the association between long noses and the ability to wield power that famous French mathematician Pascal mused that "if Cleopatra's nose had been shorter, the whole face of the earth would have been different." Doubtless, the 19th-Century concept of the "noble savage," racist as it was, hinged on a similar assessment of the Native American nose. And depictions of Jesus Christ, from Renaissance frescoes to megachurch billboards, invariably show him with a long, elegantly tapered nose that would do any Park Avenue plastic surgeon proud.

Dogs, too, follow this paradigm. Breeds that have the word "noble" in their standards — or a synonym, such as "aristocratic" or "distinguished" — invariably ask for relatively long, relatively chiseled heads and muzzles, from the Great Dane to the Doberman to the Pharaoh Hound, whose standard, not coincidentally, notes that the foreface on this breed "of noble bearing" should be slightly longer than the back skull. And let's not forget the truly Roman-nosed Borzoi, which was nurtured and perfected by Russian bluebloods, until the Bolshevik Revolution turned their own nobility into a decided liability.

Conversely, breeds with foreshortened, wide or otherwise heavy muzzles are very rarely, if ever, described as "noble" or any of its synonyms. The aforementioned Dogue, for example, is required to have a "frank" expression: unabashedly honest and serious, arguably with a bit of a curmudgeonly feel. That "sour mug" derives from the breed's distinctively set-back nose, which in turn can't exist without the correctly undershot jaw and essential upsweep of chin. And so another one of those seemingly throw-away adjectives takes us gently by the hand and leads us back to conformation and breed type.

Of course, all these visual stereotypes are just that — shorthanded assumptions that have the potential to rapidly descend into racist territory if you try to apply them literally. (The Nazis had to do some conceptual gymnastics to uphold the idea of the aquiline "Aryan" nose while at the same time vilifying that very profile in the Jews and gypsies they sought to exterminate.) But the point is not to believe that these interpretations of physical traits are correct, but rather just to understand that they existed in bygone ages, and to use that knowledge to better understand the standards we still live and breed by today.

IMHO, that is.

Bloodhound

Bichon Frisé

# Feast or Famine

*Genetics is more complex than we could ever imagine.*

When new, smart people enter the fray that we call breeding, many look with great enthusiasm to genetic testing. In an echo of the ubiquitous "There's an app for that!" when it comes to any given canine malady, the novice breeder thinks silently — or not so silently — to herself: "There's a gene for that!"

But of course, those two great humblers, time and experience, are the inevitable spoilers of such linear thinking. If only it were that easy to pinpoint a causal mutation for every ill that besets our dogs. But our dogs' genes are not static. They are evolving, dynamic and responsive to their environment — more lava lamp than laser pointer — and the emerging study of their biological capriciousness is called epigenetics.

Epigenetics explains why the genes we inherit are not always our destiny.

Why one identical twin might develop a disease that his sibling does not, or why it is impossible to clone a tortoiseshell cat and replicate its exact patterning. "Epigenetics" literally means "above genes," and when triggered by an external variable, such as diet, toxins or stress, epigenetic molecules have the power to turn genes "on" and "off." So if DNA is our body's hardware, then epigenes are its software — always changing, ready for an upgrade and, sometimes, prone to glitching.

To appreciate how daunting — or, perhaps, foolhardy — it is to presume to understand our dogs' genetic makeup, consider Överkalix.

Located just below the Arctic Circle, Överkalix is a ribbon of villages in northernmost Sweden where the population density is only six people per square mile. To survive in their subarctic climate over the centuries, Överkalix's residents fished for salmon and raised livestock, but it was their rye and barley crops that saw them through the difficult winters. Life in Överkalix could literally be feast or famine: Some years, banner crops meant that everyone gorged themselves while the wind and snow battered at their pumpkin- and ochre-colored wooden houses. But in others, the villagers were forced to fend off starvation by subsisting on small birds and the bread they made from the inner bark of fir trees.

As industrious as they were hardy, the villagers of Överkalix kept meticulous records that date back to the 15$^{th}$ Century. They recorded births and deaths; variations in health (both physical and financial), and crop yields.

Lars Olov Bygren, a preventative-health researcher at Karolinska Institute in Stockholm, was raised in Överkalix, tracing his family tree there back to 1475. Intrigued by research that showed that experiences in utero could affect a person's health as an adult, he decided to plumb the Överkalix data to see if he could find a similar ripple effect. For example, could near death from childhood starvation have a genetic impact on one's children or grandchildren?

Bygren zeroed in on the records for 1905, drawing a random sample of 99 Överkalix residents who had been born that year. Scouring the agricultural records, he and his colleagues determined how much food their fathers and grandfathers had had during their childhoods, especially during pre-puberty, when sperm cells are maturing.

The results were astounding, and more than a touch unbelievable: Boys who had experienced one of those rare winters when food was so plentiful their eating bordered on gluttonous produced sons and grandsons with shortened life expectancies. On average, the offspring of these overeaters died six years earlier — usually, of diabetes — than those whose parents and grandparents had endured food-deprived winters. When data was controlled for other factors such as socioeconomics, that number jumped to an unbelievable 32 years earlier.

So, in essence, having a grandfather who nearly died from starvation significantly increased a boy's life expectancy.

It took years for Bygren to get his paper published, not because his methodology was faulty, but because the results seemed so improbable, even impossible: It was generally accepted that epigenetics can affect how an individual's genes "behave" as they interact with the environment. But no one had posited that these changes could be passed down from generation to generation.

(Bygren's later research found that starvation had the opposite effect on women: Female residents of Överkalix who had been in utero or newly born during its years of famine — the developmental period when their ova were forming — had *deceased* life expectancy.)

How does this affect our thinking as dog breeders? Incalculably, I should think. If whether your great-grandfather ate a salami sandwich in 1898 has an impact on your longevity, think about how our animal husbandry impacts the genetic health of our breeding animals. What our dogs eat, how they are exercised, the toxins and stresses they are exposed to, and at what developmental stages — all could dramatically alter our breeding programs, for both better or worse.

It's fascinating to contemplate how this worked in the traditional, large-scale kennels of 70 or 80 years ago, when breeders reared up whole litters, and kept multiple generations under similar conditions, with identical husbandry. In such controlled, sustained environments, breeders could have unwittingly been programming their breeding programs — again, for better or worse.

There are some fanciers who like to spend their time on email lists and Facebook pages relentlessly banging the drum of how outcrossing is the only way to keep genetic disease at bay. (These pundits are usually never breeders, or in the rare case that they are, generally unsuccessful ones, though that's another story altogether.) Epigenetics is a wildcard that never factors into their pronouncements. Rather than being hyperfocused on how to avoid *expressing* a genetic problem, what a novel idea it would be to search for ways to avoid *creating* the problem in the first place.

In many ways, the more we know, the less we know. Keen breeders feel this in their bones, learning to draw as much on instinct as certificates from the Orthopedic Foundation for Animals or the University of Missouri or OptiGen. It's impossible to know what exact external forces comprise this tapestry of genetic interactions that makes our dogs who they are, but we can certainly guess. Lifestyles that most closely simulate those our dogs would experience in nature is a good starting point.

As dated or quaint as it may sound, there's real wisdom in the works of naturalists such

Airedale Terrier

Juliette de Baïracli Levy with herbs and Afghan Hounds

as the late British herbalist Juliette de Baïracli Levy, who wrote *The Complete Herbal Handbook for the Dog and Cat* in 1955. Levy bred Afghan Hounds under the Turkuman banner. Her famous export, Turkuman Nissim's Laurel, was the first Afghan to win the Hound Group at Westminster, owner-handled by Sunny Shay in 1950; when bred to the daughters of Shay's even more famous Shirkhan, he helped spark the Grandeur dynasty.

Levy, who gained her herbal knowledge from traveling with the gypsies of Europe, had a straightforward "natural rearing" philosophy: Clean food, clean water, clean air. Contact with the earth, and the sun's rays.

In her herbal handbook, Levy wrote this plea from the dog to his owner, noting that the requests were as much for health as happiness: "I pray you who own me, let me continue to live close to Nature. Know that: I love to run beneath the sun, the moon and the stars; I need to feel the storm winds around me, and the touch of rain, hail, sleet and snow; I need to splash in streams and brooks, and to swim in ponds, lakes, rivers and seas; I need to be allowed to retain my kinship with Nature.'"

Dogs reared this way — that is to say, naturally — were inherently healthier, she explained. Generations of her Turkuman Afghan Hounds thrived on it.

"Success in good health does not come overnight, it may take several generations to undo the bad health which man has been building up in his own life and the life of domestic animals during the past hundred years, when artificiality in medicine, diet and agriculture began to predominate in the Western world," she wrote. "But success, in time, is sure, because Nature's own laws are unchanging, and Nature does not fail to those who obey her simple laws."

I'll bet Juliette de Baïracli Levy didn't know about epigenetics. But her dogs — and, by extension, her breeding program — benefitted greatly nonetheless.

**Saluki**, courtesy of Mary Bloom

# How to Become a Sighthound Judge

*Or any kind of judge, really.*

What a lofty headline! Bo Bengtson, the publisher of *Sighthound Review*, where this was first printed, suggested it, and I was happy to spill out these words beneath it, though I suspect it's a little too facile in its implied sense of simply checking off boxes. Becoming anything in dogs is always a bumpy evolution.

Let's start off by making the distinction between people who judge Sighthounds and Sighthound judges. Anyone with a judging license can be the former: Here in the U.S., judges need to accumulate just 10 CEUs, or continuing education units — which are awarded for everything from attending a lure-coursing event (one CEU) to a seminar and hands-on workshop at the national specialty (a whopping three) — and they can then apply for a breed. And if that breed is deemed "low entry," like the Cirneco dell'Etna or Scottish Deerhound, for example, then all you need are five CEUs. Or even fewer, if you judge more than one group.

But a Sighthound judge is a different breed altogether. It's someone who dives deep into this family of breeds, taking the time to tease out the subtleties between them. To aspire to that level of scope in any breed is a tightrope walk: On the one hand, you want to understand a breed's nuances; on the other, you don't want to be so caught up in details that you miss the overall dog. And, to be frank, Sighthound exhibitors usually have very strong opinions, and are not always willing to extend the benefit of the doubt to those who comes from "outside" breeds. That's fair enough, and in the end, the quality of your judging will bring them round. If it doesn't, then a look in the mirror is in order.

No matter what label you apply to yourself, the process of learning about a breed — of "getting" it, in the deepest sense of the word — is as unique as a fingerprint. Some of my hardest-earned lessons were, in retrospect, plain common sense: I no longer waste time on in-ring apprenticeships with anyone whose judging I don't value in my own breed. And I don't try to learn any breed by watching a mediocre entry. (But then once those basics are learned, that mixed bag becomes invaluable in learning how to prioritize.)

Of course, there's nothing like a good mentor. Everyone says that, but the logistics are confounding, as no breed has an adequate reservoir of sages to cover its number of licensed judges. Then again, because many are content to just be judges of Sighthounds, those who aspire to be Sighthound judges can usually, with some persistence, find the feedback they need.

And feedback is always required. A fellow Hound judge offers that you need to judge at least 100 dogs of a new breed before you even know what questions to ask. (That gem was attributed to internationally respected judge Desi Murphy, who, if he didn't say it, should have.) Every breed is its own island, and when you wade ashore in the shipwreck that is your first judging assignment, you simply don't know the topography: Even the feel of the dogs beneath your hands is a new sensation. The head shape and expression and all its variations, the coat and bone and substance — all are terra incognita. It takes time to feel familiar.

I love nothing more than having one of my mentors sit ringside when I judge, and then, afterward, share his or her impressions. I always replay each assignment in my head: What better than to see it through the eyes of someone who knows the breed intimately? Because in the end, judging is about prioritizing, and the standard only provides so much guidance on that score. To fill in the blanks, you need the steadying hand of someone who has taken the breed as their own.

It's worth noting that the Doberman Pinscher Club of America has formalized this process: Permit judges — who are essentially "on probation" with the AKC until they have judged enough dogs with enough competency to be granted regular status — are observed by a member of the club's judges-education committee, who will note any glaring errors, such as rewarding a hesitant temperament. I have no idea how that works politically (don't the owners and breeders of the "wrong" dogs blow a gasket?), but it's a system that allows the club to intervene during a judge's formative assignments — and reminds the new judge that someone is watching.

No matter what the breed before her, part of the judge's role is to project a sense of omniscience: There is nothing more unsettling to exhibitors than judges who flail. Though you cannot know everything about a breed before your first assignment, you do need to walk into the ring with some type of mental scaffolding that helps you prioritize.

But, sometimes, frustratingly, the muse refuses to descend. It's at moments like those that you have to light some intellectual fires and try to smoke her out.

Consider, for example, Whippets. As my first judging assignment approached, I just didn't feel ready, and that wasn't for a lack of mentorship. So I rejiggered my schedule and drove to Maryland to attend the International Whippet Congress. I wasn't exactly sure what I was looking for, but I knew I'd know it when I saw it.

And then there it was, projected on the screen in the very first presentation, a seminar for newbies by longtime breeders Karen Lee and Iva Kimmelman called "Balance and Proportions." The slide contrasted the silhouettes of the Greyhound, Whippet and Italian Greyhound, focusing on the proportion of ribbing to loin in each: three-quarters ribs to a quarter loin in the Greyhound, two-thirds to one-third in the Whippet, and more or less equal in the IG. This was information I surely had seen elsewhere, but here it was presented at just the right time and in the right format for me to absorb it. The relationship between a Whippet's loin and its backline was now locked and loaded in my brain. Relieved, I went into that first assignment with the semblance of a clue.

That feeling of being a Hansel or Gretel without any bread crumbs to lead you can be unnerving. When I was learning Afghan Hounds, I was fortunate to have world-class mentors. And while I studied the breed, noting all its hallmark traits — the squareness, the saddle, the prominent hipbones, the croup, the ring tail, the topknot, the mandarin, and on and on — I had the persistent sense that these experts saw something I did not.

Finally, long-time Hound judge Carol Reisman flipped the switch for me. "When you see an Afghan Hound, you have to *feel* something," she explained. Feral, primitive, self-possessed — the Afghan Hound has to communicate equal parts disdain and ferocity. Or, to paraphrase world-famous Sighthound judge Espen Engh, he should look haughtily

Azawakh

Sloughi

disbelieving at the idea that you would even consider touching him, and then capable of eviscerating you should you dare try. Now, the more I judge, the more I appreciate how that exoticism is integral to the Eastern Sighthounds — Azawakhs and Salukis and the like. They have to keep that flickering flame of primitivism burning, and judges need to reward it when they see it.

Speaking of Afghan Hounds, I was lucky to watch a good portion of the national specialty several years ago with Espen. At one point we were watching a class where one dog was the clear winner — he was of superb quality, which we'll address in a second. There was a better-than-average dog to place second. But what to do for third and fourth? Which was worse — the dog with the flat croup, or the one with the tail that hit its back?

When I fretted over that dilemma, Espen dismissed it with a quote from the late judge Michele Billings.

"Don't corrupt your eye with mediocrity!" he counseled. "Look away. LOOK AWAY!"

The lesson? Obsessing over poor-quality dogs doesn't teach you anything, and in fact can set you back.

Celebrated Afghan Hound handler and now judge Michael Canalizo has always told me that a moment of truth arrives after you have been judging a new breed for a little while. At that point, if you have not botched your first assignments too badly, the more knowledgeable breeders will decide to take a chance on you. And they will bring you one of their best, a dog whose overall quality is so glaringly obvious that it will look like nothing else in the ring. That is your make-or-break moment. Fail to find that diamond amid the pebbles, and your reputation in the breed will be made — and not for the better.

It's a sad fact that show rings are filled with so many average dogs that a truly stellar one can often be dismissed as "wrong." Years ago, Borzoi breeder and judge Fred Vogel sent me a sparkling definition of quality that reinforces Michael's words, and is simply too good not to share. It was written by Elizabeth Choate, a Sealyham breeder, in 1943, but it can apply to any Sighthound, or any breed, for that matter:

*Quality is rare and is therefore highly prized. It is the outward sign of the fine heritage we strive so hard to establish in all pedigreed stock. Every once in a while, in the midst of the usual run of the mill, an animal appears with this splendid thing we call true quality. It is so fine and strong and clear that it is like a sudden bright light. It is a combination of true type, refinement and power, a symmetry of line with no modish exaggeration, encompassing the whole animal with special emphasis nowhere. Once seen in any living thing it is not forgotten, whether in man or beast.*

Let that sink in. Being able to identify that dog is the ultimate goal.

Occasionally, people ask why I decided to start judging purebred dogs. The auto-loaded answer many people give is to "improve" a given breed. That isn't my reason. (And anyway I think "improve" is the altogether wrong word: "Preserve" is much more apt.)

No, I've reached an age where I realize nothing in my life has changed much in the last quarter-century: I still have the same hairstyle, the same husband and the same home décor that I exited my thirties with. Judging lets me indulge my lifelong interest in purebred dogs, but it also forces me out of my comfort zone. It reminds me that no matter how much I know, there is so much more to learn. It reinforces the importance of humility — because there is always someone who knows more — but it also pushes you to trust your gut, your intuition, your world of wisdom within. You are there in the middle of the ring, alone, with nothing but your wits. It can be terrifying and affirming at the same time — just like life.

Judges are human, and so invariably at one time or another we notice who's on the other end of the lead. Oh, that exhibitor is … my friend … my enemy … my ex-handler … an influential fellow judge — you name it. When it comes to handing out ribbons, you might rationalize "just this once," but that is a slippery slope, and even if you are not being "officially" observed by the AKC representative, everyone is nonetheless watching: The breeders, the handlers, your fellow judges. The seasoned veterans, the rank newbies. They are watching to see what kind of judge you are. And each decision you make, each dog you point to, builds your reputation — like one of those balls they sell in stationery stores made up of thousands of individual rubber bands. Each thin circle of rubber is only strong enough to fling a paper clip, but together they form a projectile dense and powerful enough to knock you out.

Speaking of the Sighthound cognoscenti who are watching from ringside: They appreciate — no, they *expect* — a judge who knows how to approach their dogs. Never, ever, pop up from behind one of these acutely alert, visually keyed-in hunters. (I mean, they *are* Sighthounds.) If you come from a stoic breed, adjust your expectations: Pushing an unsure Sighthound puppy to the brink of hysteria will earn you no fans and possibly will wreck that youngster. The same goes for novice handlers: A few kind words and patience go a long way in welcoming newcomers to our sport.

If you judge, good luck in your transformation from simply a judge of Sighthounds to a Sighthound judge. Gramatically, that just involves moving "Sighthound" in front of "judge," but it's a bit of wordsmithing that is as symbolically powerful as it is deceptively straightforward. The dogs, after all, should always come first, both on the page and in the ring.

**Great Dane,** courtesy of Mary Bloom

# Tough Question

*An interrupted conversation continues.*

I saw the respected judge at Westminster this year sitting ringside in the front row, as befits her status in the breed she calls her own. The chair next to her was claimed with a deliberately draped jacket, but, wanting to sneak a quick visit, I took the seat, perched on its edge to communicate my transience.

Happy to see each other, as we live on opposite coasts, we chatted for a few minutes. Then I asked if I could pose a thorny question.

Her eyes twinkled, because there's nothing that pleases her more.

"Is it possible," I asked, "for a judge to stay in this game for any length of time and still maintain her integrity?"

She cocked her head, smiled, and didn't hesitate for a moment before answering.

"Yes," she replied evenly and deliberately. "But sometimes you will pay the price."

At that moment her friend returned, and I popped up with the requisite deference required of seat warmers at the Garden. "To be continued," I said over my shoulder as I hopped over legs and pocketbooks and perilously full take-out coffee cups. But I never saw her the rest of the week.

So, in her absence, I'll continue the conversation with you.

We humans are a flawed lot, as that serpent in Eden intuited all too well, and it's understandable for a judge to feel the gravitational pull of factors having nothing to do with the dogs at hand, but rather with the very human situations surrounding them. Friends, enemies, their complex hybrids the frenemies, cute little kids, imposing breed icons, the previous day's winner, proven bullies and all their endless combinations — they walk in the ring, and even if their status does not enter into a judge's final decisions, their identity is noted. How could it not be? It's human beings, not robots, who do the pointing.

Context affects judging, too. A good friend with whom I discuss dogs frequently mused about how wonderful it would be if judges could compartmentalize their judging day, so that what happened in the morning wouldn't flit across their minds, unbidden, in the afternoon. "Am I going to put another puppy from the classes to breed today?" "What will people say when I give him the breed again?"

It's a complex calculus that's fraught with assumptions: Just as exhibitors often wrongly interpret the tea leaves of judging decisions based on the limitations of their experience, so too can judges overthink what goes on in the ring. And for that we have evolutionary biology to blame: Millennia spent trying to live to see the dawn break beyond our cave entrance have wired us to analyze stressful situations to identify patterns that herald the onset of danger. (Not that I am likening the approach of an AKC rep to a saber-tooth tiger, though for some the sympathetic-nervous-system response is the same.)

Exhibitors who complain about crooked judges often have it wrong: Many adjudicators who reflexively put up "faces" do so because they are adrift. Flailing around in the whirlpool that is the show ring, they reach for the obvious lifesaver — a professional handler who is well known for having typey exhibits of a particular breed. In those cases it's not the judge's relationship with the handler that is at issue, but rather his or her relationship with the breed standard — or, more aptly, the lack of it.

Then there is the lemming effect, the mindless conga line of following what other, perhaps more respected judges have done. But what if you genuinely feel that a superstar is winning on flash instead of correctness, or just has had a supremely off day? Sometimes a valid opinion based on more than surface breed knowledge or on a dismal performance is dismissed as either ignorance or hubris. On that last score, there are judges who have anointed a particular dog and so by extension interpret any lack of acknowledgment by their peers to be a disapprobation of their own opinion. Truly, that's a no-win — in every sense of the term.

Looking up the lead for a moment, perhaps the greatest trap breeders can fall into is to correlate the success of an individual dog with their own sense of worth: It's the arc, and not any single point of its trajectory, that matters most. And so too is it with judges: In order to evolve, we must make mistakes. It is the price of admission. But it is the *kind* of mistakes that matters. Honest mistakes do not compromise integrity. In fact, they build it.

That word, integrity, was at the core of the question to my anonymous mentor. It comes from the Latin *integer*, which means "intact" and is closely related to the word "entirety." And that makes perfect sense: Judges with integrity practice a wholeness of self, resisting the impulse to allow external influences to dominate their decision-making. And isn't that what we're all striving for, on many levels — completeness?

That is, after all, what we ask of the dogs in front of us: We want them to be of a piece, cut out of whole cloth. We don't want any individual component to detract from the big picture; instead, the whole should transcend the sum of its parts.

That describes a good judge, too. We all have different parts of us, in terms of experience, perspective and relationships. They make us who we are — individual masterpieces, not cheap photocopies. A judge with integrity, with wholeness, strives to move forward in the ring as the tapestry that she is, not allowing one factor or another to dominate.

Not everyone judges that way, to be sure, and perhaps that's for the best. As one kennel-club higher-up told me with the threat of imminent death should I ever attribute it, bad judges — whether that adjective derives from politics or incompetence — have their place, too. Otherwise, the same obviously correct dogs would win most of the time, and everyone else would soon learn to stay home.

Returning to that short-lived Westminster interlude, there is indeed a price to be paid for ignoring the inevitable politics in the ring. The show chair who was out of the ribbons likely now isn't going to give you that coveted assignment. That influential handler may make it his life mission to ensure you never judge his hometown show ever again. And the AKC rep may endure a foot-tappingly long line of exhibitors griping that your penchant for consistency meant that the same kennel took home every plum to be plucked.

But arguably the more you act out of integrity, the more people will come to expect it, and so will not bridle as often when you are true to yourself. You will sit in your hard-earned ringside seat confidently and comfortably, not perched on the edge of indecision, waiting for someone else's agenda to determine your vantage point. And you can continue on with the business of learning, occasionally stumbling but always evolving, with the delicious result of becoming ever more complete.

**Komondor**, courtesy of Mary Bloom

Frau Stockmann and early vom Dom Boxers.

# Forgotten Voices

*Remembering Frau Stockmann of Boxer fame.*

If you are an ardent student of dogs, the universe never dodges the opportunity to show you how much you don't know.

Enter Friederun von Miram-Stockmann.

On a whim, a good friend suggested I pick up a copy of Frau Stockmann's 1960 memoir, *Ein Leben mit Boxern*, which translates into English as *My Life With Boxers*. It has been out of print for years, and I had no idea who Stockmann was. But, knowing this good dog man would never lead me astray, I scored a used copy on Amazon and settled in.

Hopefully many in the American dog fancy have at least heard the name Ch. Bang Away of Sirrah Crest, the inimitable Boxer who dominated dog shows for much of the 1950s. Bang Away was, quite simply, "the greatest American Boxer of all time," says the American Boxer Club website, noting that he was "the Boxer who won the most, sired the most champions and changed the look of the breed."

But what many don't know is that without the hard work of this matronly artist eking out a living on a supposedly accursed Bavarian farm, there would have been no Bang Away, and the trajectory of the American Boxer would have been irrevocably altered.

It almost shortchanges Stockmann to call her a master breeder, because she was so much more. Pat Trotter, who has written extensively about Stockmann and her vom Dom dogs, considers her "the greatest, most influential dog breeder of them all." Stockmann standardized the Boxer at a time when type was still in flux and the fire of its forbearer, the Bullenbeisser — literally, "bull biter" — still smoldered. And after a lifetime in the breed Stockmann also perfected it, creating a family of impeccably line-bred Boxers whose beauty and prepotency were soon sought after by dollar-waving Americans in the lull between the two world wars.

Born in 1891 in Latvia to ethnic Germans, Stockmann read about the Boxer after sneaking in her brother's bedroom at night to filch his boy's almanac. Later, encouraged by her mother to take art classes in Munich, she met a fellow student with a slight limp who explained that his boisterous dog — with "a big head, a black face and a coat like a tiger" — had joyfully bowled him over and down the stairs. In due course, master and dog alike stole Stockmann's heart.

Stockmann wrote *My Life With Boxers* while in her 70s, and the book chronicles her personal evolution. She starts off constrained by Victorian mores, helpless in the face of that new Boxer's bloodthirst: On walks, her muzzled Pluto would "jump the first big dog he saw," putting his face near his combatant's so the muzzle would be ripped off and leave Pluto free to use his teeth, which he did — gleefully.

Similarly, Stockmann chronicles her growth as a breeder. As she studies the magazine published by the Munich Boxer club, she begins to see Pluto with new eyes. "Where did my ideal dog go? There was a great separation between the desired image of a Boxer and mine," she writes. "Why, I asked myself, is a short back nicer than a long one? Why do the legs have to appear to be straight when viewed from the side? Were these merely the opinions of others whose dogs happened to look like that?"

**Ch. Bang Away of Sirrah Crest**, courtesy AKC Museum of the Dog

Later, she finds her answer: "Everything which best fulfills a purpose is also beautiful."

Flinging herself into the breed, Stockmann begins breeding under her famous affix, vom Dom — literally, "from the cathedral" — and encounters setbacks that are all too familiar to breeders: tragic deaths, outbreaks of disease, failed breedings and disappointing litters.

When the pick male from her first litter does not turn out, "I began to think that it would not be easy to breed the ideal Boxer," Stockmann muses. "Who knows how long it would have taken if I had not been lucky? Over and over I have learned that knowledge and superiority will not do it if you have bad luck. But there isn't such thing as eternal good luck either."

Stockmann had good luck, all right — ensconced within a heaping dose of bad. As World War I settles over her kennel, her husband Philipp Stockmann — he of the long-ago limp — is conscripted into the German army, as are 10 of her dogs, including her first influential stud, Rolf vom Vogelsberg.

Left alone to care for her dogs and infant daughter, Stockmann embarks on an endless search for kennel feed — pedaling dozens of miles on a bicycle with tarred tires to drag home buckets of cow intestines.

Even more unsettling is the reader's realization that a second world war, exponentially more cruel and debilitating, looms on the horizon. By then, Stockmann is reduced to buying the carcasses of old dogs from farmers, though her starving ones are so adverse to eating their own that she obliterates the taste with heaps of seasonings.

All great breeders reject convention, and so too did Stockmann. She writes about her foray into the black Boxer, which initially derived, she openly admits, from a Bulldog-Schnauzer cross. In defiance of the Munich Boxer Club, she breeds a litter, experiments with using black shoe polish to augment the coat, and even takes some into the ring, though the judges balk at her innovation. Similarly intrigued, she attempts to crossbreed dogs with red foxes, though she eventually gives up on these "shy biting bachelors," who gnawed through stone walls to escape their captivity.

There are endless tidbits throughout the book, melting into a reader's consciousness like those delicious chocolate-marizpan Mozartkugels of which Bavarians are so fond. Stockmann was the first to use the convention of naming a litter for a consecutive letter of the alphabet, still common today, especially in Europe. Partial to brindles, which she felt "were more noble and had better heads" (though they could be "rather homely" if plain, she admits), Stockmann also valued fawns for their "superior structure," in particular good top lines and rear angles. And her cutting description of a ring full of mediocre dogs — "a bunch of pathetic witnesses to a lost glory" — applies, ruefully, to many lackluster entries today.

While Stockmann is sentimental about her dogs, she makes hard decisions to push her line forward. That is clear at the outset, when she places Pluto in order to acquire the conformationally superior Rolf, though she senses that the fates will eventually extract a price for that betrayal. And they do.

With dozens of dogs to feed, relying on the yields of her farm and her wood carvings to earn a living, Stockmann invariably finds herself in precarious financial straits. But as her reputation grows, there are well-off fanciers with wads of cash willing to take dogs off her hands.

On the eve of World War II, with the Nazi regime micromanaging her agricultural affairs and an unknown disease sweeping through her farm, Stockmann accepts an unprecedented sum of 11,000 marks for her beloved Lustig vom Dom — "the sunshine of our home." Though the sale enables her to buy a car — whose batteries and tires the Nazis eventually confiscate anyway — she immediately regrets it.

"A thousand thoughts raced through my grieving mind," she writes. "I even seriously considered pulling off a swindle and shipping another dog. Who would know the difference? Who knew in America, where Lustig was going, just what he looked like? The

Stockmann exhibiting Lustig vom Dom

broker who bought him knew nothing. I could … I could paint more markings on Lustig and hide him for the rest of his life. Or maybe it would be possible to follow Lustig's crate and release him at night from his strange kennel. One call from me, and there wouldn't be a fence high enough to keep him from my side."

Too distraught to take him to the train station, Stockmann sends her daughter. The grand Boxer, wearing a collar that reads *Ich Bin Der Herrliche Lustig* ("I am the magnificent Lustig"), looks out pleadingly from the crate, his leash in his mouth, anticipating his fate.

Stockmann's sacrifice — one of many — was America's gain. Lustig — together with his younger brother Utz vom Dom; their stunning grandfather Sigurd vom Dom; and another Sigurd grandson, the brindle Dorian vom Marienhof — comprise the "Four Horsemen" of the Boxer in America. Rather than an apocalypse, they brought the transformation of the breed into the peerlessly elegant showman we have today.

At the end of the war — and the book — Stockmann is invited to America by wealthy and eager Boxer fanciers. Unable to speak much English, squired around to all the prominent East Coast kennels, she experiences culture shock at the preponderance of everything American — cars, lush lawns, makeup, air conditioning, buffet lunches. Flown to California — add palm trees and ocean views to that list — she judges a match show of 90 puppies.

"Among the males, a little fellow immediately caught my eye, a fawn with white markings and white socks. That's Lustig, I thought," she remembers. "But a closer look showed that he was not quite the same. Lustig was more powerful, his head more sharply chiseled. Yet the grand pose and the long graceful neck brought back memories of this puppy's great ancestor."

Yes, the puppy that Stockmann dubbed "little Lustig" — and the winner of that match — was none other than Bang Away. And her assessment encapsulated both macro and micro: Bang Away's sound and elegant style went on to define Boxer type in America, although he had his faults, nonetheless carrying them extraordinarily well. (In her *Born to Win* book, Pat Trotter tactfully notes that "he did his best producing when bred to bitches with strong heads behind them.")

Stockmann never saw Lustig again, though her husband did: He judged at Westminster a year after Lustig was exported, awarding him Best of Breed.

"He ended his show career after that," Stockmann writes of Lustig. "In America, he will remain immortal, because the Americans value tradition much more than we do."

Immortality, however, requires repetition, and repetition requires telling. And so now, if you've read this far, I have done my small part.

French Bulldog

# The Flutter of Familiarity

*Close encounters of the breeding kind.*

We take our breeds with us.

Not literally, of course, sliming up the back window of the SUV or whimpering under the airplane seat. No, we carry our breeds inside us. And sometimes when we see a different breed, our original one stirs, as if we've just opened the refrigerator door amid a pack of snoozing housedogs.

If I had to identify the place that feeling manifests, it would be midway between sternum and navel, a tender little spot that feels a tug when your eye alights on something that evokes your breed.

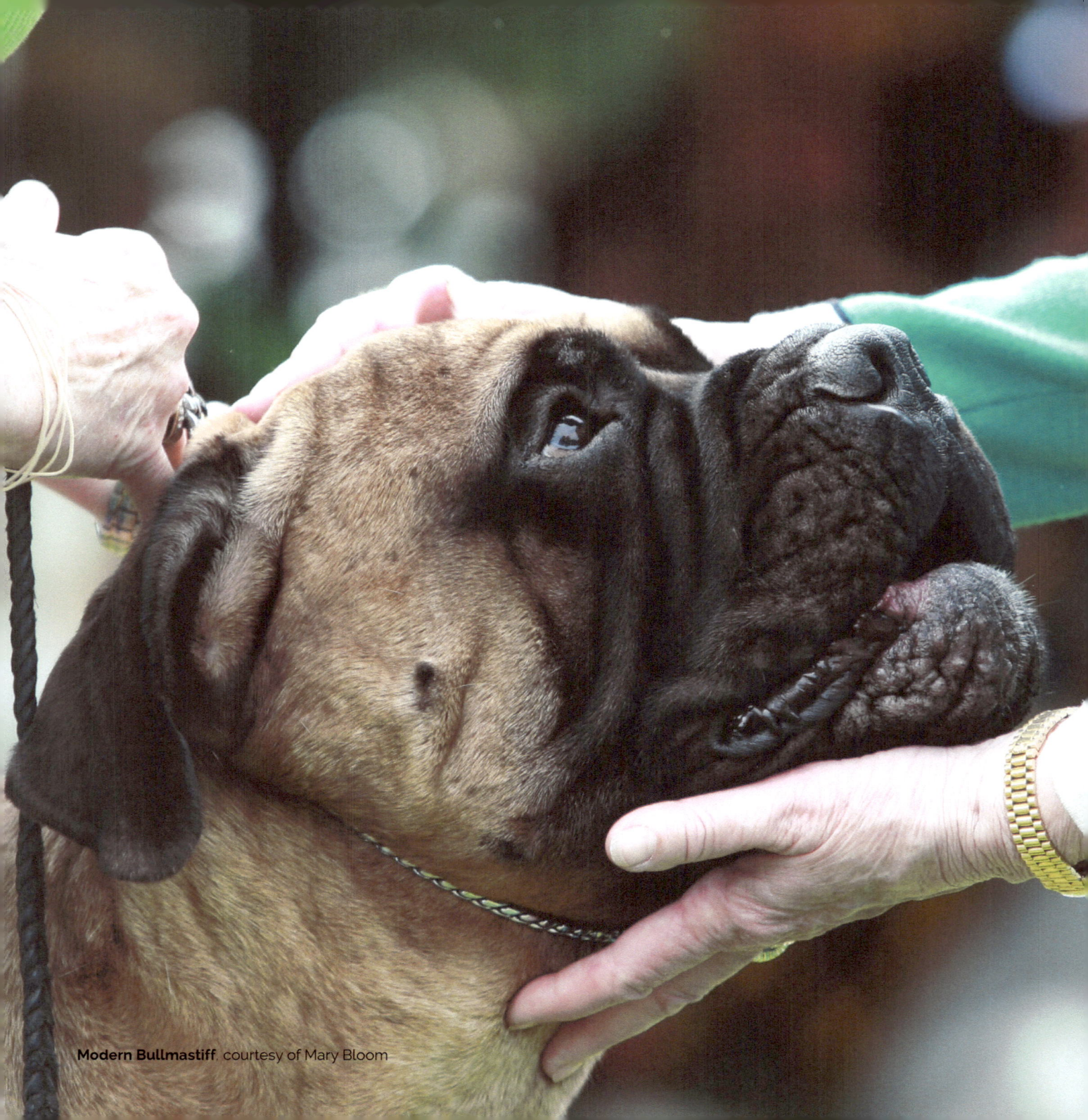
**Modern Bullmastiff**, courtesy of Mary Bloom

I always experience that flutter of familiarity when I attend a Bullmastiff national. Invariably, I'll scan the lineup of a sweepstakes class, and my eye will screech to a halt on a youngster who is hypotypical — that is, lacking in type. He will be lighter in bone, too long cast, with a slightly longer muzzle and a lot of air under him. He attracts me not because he is correct — quite the

**Early Bullmastiff, Roger of the Fenns**

opposite — but because he is familiar. He evokes my breed — the Rhodesian Ridgeback — which in the Bullmastiff ring is decidedly not a good thing.

From a historical perspective, this is not accidental. Though Bullmastiffs are not mentioned in the Ridgeback creation story that has been handed down to fanciers over the years, recent studies have found that the two breeds have a genetic link. And since the famous de Beers diamond mines were known to have purchased and even registered both breeds, the opportunity for cross-pollination certainly existed. Roger of the Fenns, a Bullmastiff from the 1930s who was so influential virtually every modern Bullmastiff goes back to him, could easily be mistaken for an overdone Ridgeback today.

Back to that gravitational pull: It's unbidden, reflexive. And that's understandable, given how deeply we know the breed to which we have devoted ourselves.

Metaphorically speaking, your breed is like your house: You've internalized its quirks and idiosyncrasies. You know which staircase treads to avoid so they don't creak, or how long to shower before the hot-water heater wavers in its commitment, or how to jiggle the handle of the temperamental second-floor toilet just so. In fact, you've done these things for so long and so often that you no longer think about them. You're on automatic pilot.

Contrast that to the house of a generous friend who lets you stay over while he's out of town. You fumble with the balky lock, feel around in the dark in search of the hallway light switch, contemplate the kitchen cupboards to divine where the coffee mugs are. You are very acutely aware of how much you don't know. But if somewhere in this strange terrain you come upon something that your house shares — even something as basic as the same Keurig coffee maker — here comes that flutter of familiarity.

The most important thing to realize about this sensation is that it is extremely pleasant because it provides relief in a situation where you are besieged by the unfamiliar. If we are talking about your friend's house, the end result is an expertly made cup of Green Mountain breakfast blend. But if we are in the dog-show ring, the results can be ruinous.

That's because the operant four-letter word for maintaining high quality in purebred dogs is type. By definition, type encompasses all those attributes that make a breed unique. Once a trait from another breed takes hold — what the late, great judge Anne Rogers Clark called the "drag" of the breed — then it's time to call 911.

It's the judge's job, then, to disregard that flash of familiarity when it bubbles up, which is easier said than done. Because the first step is just realizing that it is happening.

Judging a breed different from your own is often an uncomfortable feeling, the doggy version of an itchy wool sweater. The less familiar you are at first, the more adrift you feel. Reading and studying a standard is all well and good, but formulating the mental scaffolding you need to truly understand a breed takes time and patience. Sometimes it's just easier to follow that flutter of familiarity where it leads you, even if it's entirely wrong.

Arguably the better choice, if the more difficult one, is to clearly, consciously and perhaps forcibly reject that sense of doggie déjà vu and the security it represents, opting instead to delve more deeply into the breed at hand. While it will never be as familiar as your own, you can eventually get to a place where you understand it well enough to manage all the basics — the alarm system, the satellite TV and that good old Keurig, to return to our house metaphor.

At some point, that new breed may trigger its own smaller, stiller but still discernible flutters of familiarity in you when you are looking at yet another breed. You just may not feel it as viscerally as you do with your own.

As for that breed that first claimed you, and which chances are brought you to the sport of purebred dogs, leave it where it belongs — in your house, and heart.

Chinese Crested

# In Defense of Beauty

*It's more than skin deep.*

Don't hate me because I'm beautiful.

If our purebred dogs could talk, they'd likely mouth that 1980s catchphrase from model Kelly LeBrock. Granted, her television ads pimped Pantene shampoo, but the parallel still holds: In much of our popular culture, our purebreds are dismissed as airheaded Adonises, our dog shows as misguided beauty pageants.

The cultural conclusion is clear: Producing beauty for beauty's sake is somehow morally lacking, a whimsical extravagance, a misplaced priority.

Many years ago, I read an essay on the website of a Canadian breeder who had Schnauzers. That's all I remember about her: The internet seems to have swallowed up her website, Jonas-in-the-whale style. Her argument, however, has stayed with me: Many things can challenge breeders in their programs, including iffy temperaments and health problems. But the one thing that will hasten a kennel's demise is the inability to produce attractive animals. Simply put, no one wants or values a line of consistently ugly dogs.

The natural world offers plenty of examples of what appears to be beauty for beauty's sake: the ostentatious plumage of the peacock, the bright, ribbon-like tail feathers of the bird-of-paradise. In dogs, we breeders tug the genetic marionette strings, shortening a foreface here, growing more coat there. But what is the driving force in nature?

A fascinating answer — or, more accurately, series of unresolved answers — appears in a recent *New York Times Magazine* article by Ferris Jabr titled "Beauty and the Beasts." It tackles a thorny question: Is the "extravagant splendor" of the animal kingdom intentional or arbitrary?

Jabr explains that going as far back as Charles Darwin, scientists debated the "evolutionary justification" for beautiful plumage that compromised a bird's camouflage, or elaborate mating dances and rituals that burned much-needed calories.

One theory espoused by many biologists is that this dramatic ornamentation is a "code" for unseen, genetically transmitted qualities — signaling that a prospective mate has more vigorous health, higher intelligence or better overall survival qualities, all of which would benefit future offspring. In other words, beautiful on the outside translates to beautiful on the inside, in a genetic sense.

For his part, Darwin rejected this explanation, arguing that in a process called "sexual selection," females of a species gravitated toward males with over-the-top ornamentation "according to their standard of beauty," and that males in turn evolved to display those characteristics, no matter how arbitrary or even deleterious to their survival. Jabr notes that many Victorian academics scoffed at Darwin's premise: How could what one of his contemporaries called "vicious feminine caprice" possibly impact a species' evolution?

"Darwin did not think it was necessary to link aesthetics and survival," Jabr writes. "Animals, he believed, could appreciate beauty for its own sake."

Today, some modern scientists have rediscovered and embraced Darwin's theory. "Beauty, they say, does not have to be a proxy for health or advantageous genes. Sometimes beauty is the glorious but meaningless flowering of arbitrary preference," Jabr continues. "Animals simply find certain features — a blush of red, a feathered flourish — to be appealing. And that innate sense of beauty itself can become an engine of evolution, pushing animals toward aesthetic extremes. In other cases, certain environmental or physiological constraints steer an animal toward an aesthetic preference that has nothing to do with survival whatsoever."

That perspective begs the question: Where does an animal derive its sense of aesthetics?

Jabr finds that answer among neurobiologists, who study why a certain type of bird song or fin color triggers interest in a potential mate. This "sensory bias," he explains, is the result of not just an animal's environment, but how its biology responds to it. One fish species might be attracted to a certain color because of the light levels in the water depths in which they swim; some frogs might respond to a particular mating call because they evolved the ability to hear that frequency for some long-ago purpose, and as a result it penetrates their awareness more sharply than other equally pleasing sounds.

When it comes to our purposefully bred dogs, Jabr's article invites many layers of questions. Evolutionary biologists speculate that we humans are hard-wired to be attracted to neonatal, or baby-like, features, like large heads and eyes, flat faces and short limbs, so much so that they override the physical and emotional cost of rearing our own young: Cuteness, they argue, is an effective vaccination against infanticide. It's not a far leap, then, to understanding the appeal of breeds as diverse as the Pug and Basset Hound.

Fair enough. But what about the wrinkled face of the Mastiff, or the curled tail of the Basenji, or the spotted white coat of the Dalmatian? As Jabr explains, because our ideas of beauty are a balancing act between caprice and intention, inspiration and function, we may never know exactly why. Like some people's Facebook status, it's *complicated*.

America's roots are in the asceticism of the Puritans, for whom the idea of beauty before utility was nothing short of sacrilege. We carry that into our animal husbandry, which is

Cardigan Welsh Corgi

why modern culture today often derides breeders for breeding for beauty. (Contrast that to cultures in which beauty is valued and vaunted: Is it a coincidence that the Italians developed the world's most operatic breed, the Neapolitan Mastiff?) But if, as Jabr argues, nature itself values beauty so much that it is willing to trade a bit of survivability in to-hell-with-camouflage creatures such as the plum-throated cotinga or the peacock spider, then why not accept a range of features in our purebred dogs, so long as their soundness is not unduly compromised?

Science shows us that beauty for beauty's sake is hard wired in us, as it is with so many other species, from mammals to insects. And it turns out that in the end, our dog breeds, in all their diversity, are merely a reflection of both our individual and evolutionary selves, our desire for symmetry and novelty and striking sizes, shapes and colors.

In the wild, when excessive form pushes function to the wall, natural selection is the final arbiter: If a trait is too disadvantageous, the organism simply does not survive. In the whelping box and beyond, breeders have the ability circumvent nature's cruel culling — those marionette strings again — with medical and veterinary intervention.

So there you have it, the boundaries for our purebred pursuit of beauty: It is perfectly acceptable — even part of our neurobiological wiring — to perpetuate a trait simply because it pleases us aesthetically, even if there is no function to "justify" it. But when that pursuit of beauty pushes the envelope so far that it sails off the table, then we have gone too far.

So there is no shame in that shiver of pleasure you feel when you see a beautifully arched neck, or dark, trusting spaniel eye, or silky, flowing coat. No, to recast that decades-old advertising slogan, love them because they *are* beautiful. It's what nature would have you do.

Nova Scotia Duck Tolling Retriever

# Present Company

*How big is your breed's tent?*

You never know what people will object to.

Recently, I wrote about an unusual coat color that has cropped up in a particular breed.

"Standards are, by definition, about exclusion. As breeds evolve and solidify, they begin to tighten the noose of type," the article began. "And, sometimes, the written standard becomes the order of execution for certain traits, whether it's a particular ear carriage or size or color — usually something connected to another breed that was introduced in the foundation period. Years or decades later, these purged characteristics can resurface, perplexing breeders and prompting some fanciers to ask why they were excluded in the first place."

In an email after the story was published, a reader — but not a breeder nor judge — took exception to those opening words.

"I strongly disagree that a standard is there for exclusion," the email concluded. "A standard is there to identify the breed characteristics."

I didn't answer the email, but I knew what I would have said if I did: In order to know a thing, we need to know its opposite. The concept of light is meaningless without an understanding of darkness, and so it is with inclusion and exclusion. The glass is both half full and half empty. It all depends on your vantage point.

But my own perspective had been challenged by that email. By thinking of breeds in terms of what to keep out rather than what to keep in, was I committing the same sin as the judge who rejects a dog for its faults rather than rewarding its virtues?

Then, stepping back a bit further, was there a cultural lesson here? Is this why the sport of dogs has such a disconnect with the popular culture? In our fragmented political times, is a process that highlights the tribalism among breeds like adding gasoline to the fire?

At first blush, looking at the format of a breed standard didn't seem to support my view. Standards for the most part describe what is desired in a breed rather than what's not. While faults and sometimes disqualifications are mentioned, they are very much in the minority.

But breed standards aren't static documents. Like breeds themselves, they evolve, and that progression is a funnel, moving from a state of diversity to one of greater homogeny.

If I think back to the evolution of my own breed and its standard, everything from the permissible colors and patterns to its hallmark trait grew more and more specific with time — and with each new iteration of the standard. Where once Ridgebacks had sables and whole colors with white and brindles and fawns, now we have only wheatens. Where once we had ridges of every shape and configuration — some doing a serviceable impression of a Rorschach test — now we have the sword-shaped stripe of backward-growing hair with two crowns that are directly opposite each other and positioned within the top third of the ridge.

Ever more specific and exclusionary? Doubtless. So what I wrote was true. But — and this is a different question altogether — was it *right*?

Like it or not, animal breeding today is seen through a complex social matrix. Increasingly, breeders are cast as Nazis; our selection process is compared to eugenics and our breeds to the quest for master races. When I wince a bit at the word exclusion, is it because our richly diverse American culture is one of inclusion? Am I rejecting the melting pot?

The difference, of course, is that cultures are supposed to grow and expand, unless they are in a state of decline. (See: Rome, Ancient.) In this respect they are like the universe — ever expanding, ever diversifying. But dog breeds are more like supernovae, contracting into themselves as they mature.

After all, the vast majority of our dog breeds are the result of a culture or nation that outgrew an earlier idiom: The native people who relied on the Samoyed now have snowmobiles, the Otterhound's traditional prey is endangered and legally protected, and the Ridgeback's big-game hunting role went out with the ox-pulled wagon. Breeds are innately retrospective, which is why we have embraced the label of *preservation* breeders.

Come to think of it, there's already a name for a group of related dogs among whom inclusion is the dominant paradigm. It's called a land race.

By their very definition, land races are not fixed. They allow for a great deal of diversity. They don't fit our modern definition of a breed specifically because they are too diffused.

Seeing the glass as half full as opposed to half empty can also be pragmatically challenging in the whelping box. It's not enough to choose dogs that have the traits we want, from good fronts to correct outlines. We also have to vigorously reject those traits that are the drag of the breed — remnants of a contributing founder, or a cross done to add one desired quality, but that brought with it a half-dozen unwanted ones.

That's not to say that this exclusionary focus in purebred dogs is incompatible with genetic diversity. Indeed, we need *more* dogs being bred, not fewer, though that also runs afoul of social mores.

Sometimes, when I judge certain breeds, I am confronted with an entry that evokes anything but the one listed on the schedule posted at the entrance to the ring. I think rather than passing out ribbons, I should be conducting an exorcism, so unwelcome and unsettling are these heads and bodies that don't belong to the breed whose label they bear. After all, what's the point of an Irish Wolfhound that looks like a Scottish Deerhound, or a Siberian Husky that brings to mind an Alaskan Malamute?

There's only one thing that prevents such cases of mistaken identity from occurring. It's having the discipline to exercise exclusion — in both breeding and showing. After all, if a dog belongs to a breed on paper, but it doesn't look like the breed, or behave like the breed, is it conceptually part of that breed — or on its way to being something else?

As koans go, that's one for the Dalai Lama.

White Bull Terrier

Dogue de Bordeaux courtesy of Sanna Sander

# Getting Critical

*The art — and artifice — of writing judging critiques.*

It's not what you say. It really is how you say it.

Unlike some of my fellow American dog-show judges, I like doing critiques, which are a requirement if ever you judge abroad. After all, I like to write — otherwise you'd be reading someone else's book — and I can usually string a serviceable sentence together. But writing good critiques isn't about grammar or conjugation. It's about knowing how to say something gently enough so that it can be heard without the whiplash of indignation that most fanciers suffer at even the mildest criticism of the dog at the end of their lead. Getting *triggered,* my kids call it.

Two years ago, at the famous Bucks County Kennel Club show in tulip-suffused Pennsylvania, I spent a couple of pleasant hours with a gaggle of Dogues de

Bordeaux. One of my mentors in the breed, Bas Bosch of Belgium, had judged them that day, and afterward was offering individual critiques. Graciously, he allowed me to listen as he dictated his comments to a transcriber, who typed them into the laptop perched atop her knees. It was my second time eavesdropping on his spoken critiques, but the first time since I had started judging, so my interest was even more piqued.

One after another the Dogues came, and with each, Bas followed a similar format: First, the overall impression. Then, the individual aspects of conformation, starting at the nose and ending at the tail. And, finally, comments on movement and temperament.

Though Bas is from the Continent, he is of the English school, which is to say he can deliver the most soul-crushing critique with words as velvety as rose petals. If you understand your breed, then you leave with the feeling that an evenhanded appraisal has been delivered as diplomatically as possible. And if you *really* understand your breed, you knew your dog's faults anyway. But if you have no clue, you're still quite satisfied, as the word picture sounds so very pleasant.

As the critiques rolled on, I began decoding the language. Less-than-stellar conformation earned the adjective "decent"; so, for example, a straight-fronted dog had "decent angulation." Negative attributes were always cast positively, in the conditional tense: Never "cow hocked," but rather the demure "would prefer," as in "would prefer a lower hock."

The English are, of course, masters of this iron-fist-in-velvet-glove commentary. Inspired, I started Googling the critiques of well-regarded UK judges such as Zena Thorne-Andrews, who is Britain's only all-rounder, and sporting-dog icon Frank Kane. In their critiques, a dog didn't have a gay tail: He was just "proud" of it. A bitch wasn't pushing the top of the standard; she was instead "at full measure for size." In the English critiques

I found clever adjectives to use in place of the far more negative ones ping-ponging inside my head. A common, plain dog was "workmanlike" or "honest." If he was a bit too much dog, there was "no mistaking his sex." In a nod to good handling, a dog was "shown to advantage."

And, as one of my English mentors in my own breed explained to me, you can always say something nice about a dog's temperament: "stable," "unflappable," "easygoing." For those dogs who think they are seeing dead people, there's "a bit unsettled on the day" or "not making the best of himself."

Some of the cleverest euphemisms are the ones Bas coined himself. Back at those Dogue appraisals, a lovely bitch was next in line. She was noticeably overweight. No one likes to be called fat, and no one likes it when their dog is called that, either.

Bas didn't skip a beat. "A bit *rich in condition*," he dictated.

Now, if there is a Best in Show critique phrase, it's calling a fat show dog "rich in condition."

Later on, Bas encountered a Dogue with flyaway ears — a frustrating problem in triangular-eared breeds like Bullmastiffs and Ridgebacks, whose ears can crimp, "Flying Nun" style, during teething and will stay that way unless corrected, usually with taping.

"Ear carriage a bit *untidy*," he noted, firing off another original.

A couple of years later, while judging a Rhodesian Ridgeback club show in Italy, I had the chance to craft a euphemism of my own. In the baby puppy class, I had a bitch with weepy eyes, which made me concerned they might be entropic. I needed to note the anomaly, but wanted to be subtle about it.

"Eyes a bit *misty*," I told my befuddled scribe, Giuseppe. Once the critiques were distributed, some of the Italians huddled over their smart phones to consult Google Translate. "Ahhh, *si*, like Misty Meadows," said the curious representative from the Italian kennel club when I explained the meaning, referencing the famous Chihuahua kennel now based outside of Rome.

All these verbal gymnastics might seem like a self-indulgent parlor game, or a misguided attempt to sugarcoat the truth in a sport where real connoisseurs are evaporating at an alarming pace. But when seemingly every other article in dog-show publications bemoans the graying of the sport, the insularity of our culture and the difficulty newcomers experience as a result, I can't imagine that a gentle — not to mention genteel — approach can do harm. If just one fancier does a bit more research or asks a question as a result of a critique whose salient points seem at first a bit, well, *misty*, then I count that as a success.

And, hopefully, the ability to interpret those words improves over time. Sometimes, we just can't handle the truth from where we are standing, so blinded are we by our own prejudices, or lack of knowledge. But just as returning to a good book after some time has passed gives you fresh insight — or lets you see what you completely overlooked before — perhaps tincture of time works the same way with critiques, too.

At one point that afternoon, Bas was presented with what he would call, tongue planted firmly in cheek, a "Bordino" — a sly portmanteau describing a Bordeaux that has too many of the traits of a *mastino*, or Neapolitan Mastiff.

Carefully and clearly, Bas pointed out all the aspects of type that pushed this dog from Dogue territory to Neo wannabe: the relatively flat ribcage, straighter topline, more upstanding presence and the excess of lip and wrinkle, especially the fold that runs from

Rhodesian Ridgeback

Border Collie

the inner corner of the eye to the commissure of the mouth — required in a Neo but anathema in the Dogue, whose FCI standard insists that specific wrinkle be "discreet." This dog's wrinkles were about as discreet as Roseanne Barr.

"I just love his wrinkles, too!" exclaimed the owner as she read through the critique, clearly pleased as punch. "It makes him look like a teddy bear!"

Will that owner one day return to that scrap of paper and see those words as they were intended — as a call for correction, not a compliment? Who knows. But if she does ever re-read it, the deeper meaning will await her. After all, writing and judging are in the end interactive endeavors — writers write so they will be read, and judges judge so that their opinions can be contemplated.

But if the words, like some great dogs, are a bit ahead of their time, at least as far as the recipient goes, then having a clueless exhibitor depart while gleefully hugging her teddy bear seems to me a misunderstanding worth accepting.

Labradoodle

# What's in Your Genes?

*Hybrid vigor — and the road to get there.*

It isn't very often that you come across a book about the breeding of our own species. After all, most of us are "random bred": With the relatively rare exception of arranged marriages, pairings of human sires and dams are pretty arbitrary, based on whim, serendipity and, sometimes, one too many Cosmopolitans.

Which is why I was intrigued when I came across *Breeding Between the Lines: Why Interracial People Are Healthier and More Attractive* (Barricade Books, 2006). Given the title, I knew this wasn't going to be a celebration of carefully circumscribed gene pools, like the ones that define our purebred dogs (or any other purposefully bred animal, for that matter). I had an idea of what I was in for: Hybrid vigor = good. Inbreeding = bad. But, my curiosity piqued, I ordered it on Amazon.

Ironically, author Alon Ziv comes from a rather closed pedigree himself: His father has Gaucher disease, a recessive genetic disorder common among Jews of European origin in which the body fails to produce an enzyme needed for the breakdown of fats. Because their religion proscribes marriage to outsiders, Ashkenazi Jews have a higher-than-average carrier rate of Gaucher disease (almost 9 percent, compared to 1 percent of all Americans). But what's interesting about Ziv's book is not the inevitable indictment of "breeding close," but rather his arguments in favor of outcrossing — or, in human terms, intermarriage.

In his book — which is peppered, sometimes distractingly, with pop-culture references, from J. Lo to Tiger Woods — Ziv spends a great deal of time discussing symmetry. Since antiquity, human culture has equated symmetry with beauty. Think of Leonardo da Vinci's Vitruvian Man, the 15$^{th}$-Century drawing of a male nude superimposed in itself and inscribed within a circle and a square, symbolic of the symmetry of the human body, and the universe beyond. We like mirror images — two arms, two legs, two breasts, and so it goes. The more visually balanced something — or someone — is, the more attractive we find it.

This isn't just aesthetics, Ziv argues: It is biological imperative. Trotting out a zoo's worth of examples — cheetahs, tamarin monkeys, rainbow trout, house sparrows, thoroughbred horses, side-blotched lizards — Ziv makes the argument that symmetrical organisms are not just more attractive, but are also healthier. And here is the genetic kicker: The more heterozygous an individual is, the more likely he or she is to be symmetrical. (For those who aren't genetics buffs, in its simplest terms, "heterozygous" refers to being more genetically diverse, and less inbred.)

Ziv's argument, then, is that the more inbred you are, the less likely you are to be symmetrical, and therefore the less likely you are to be healthy. And well-being — which in the statistics he gathers encompasses, among other things, higher disease and parasite resistance, fertility, athleticism, growth rates and social extroversion — isn't the only benefit of being symmetrical: Ziv sites studies that show that symmetrical men lose their virginity three to four years earlier than their more lopsided peers, and have two to three times more sex partners; for their part, women with more symmetrical sex partners were much more likely to climax during sex. (And you thought it was his cologne.)

Ziv posits that the two most unrelated human groups on the planet are the Bantu of South Africa and the Eskimos of northernmost North America; a marriage between members of these two groups, he theorizes, would produce the greatest heterozygosity. And the greater the heterozygosity, the more likely you are to be healthier and better equipped to survive and pass your genes on to the next generation.

Ziv points out that farmers have long known this to be true, as hybrid crosses in agriculture demonstrate. Crossing two unrelated strains of inbred corn gives farmers hybrid seeds that produce hardy, high-yield crops. The disadvantage to this, of course, is that the hybrid seed has to be re-created with every generation.

It doesn't take very long for this to segue to purebred dogs, with "designer dogs" as the corresponding model.

"Although hybrid corn and Labradoodles don't appear to have a lot in common, their genetic history is comparable," Ziv writes. "All our examples of hybrid vigor follow a similar pattern. Two or more strains or variants are created by inbreeding a small number of individuals. These strains are kept separate and only breed among themselves."

As politically incorrect as it is to compare dogs and humans in terms of "crossing breeds," Ziv nonetheless does it. "Mixing two different inbred strains leads to hybrid vigor whether you're talking about wheat, dogs or humans," he concludes. "It's as simple as that."

It's easy to walk away from Ziv's book dismissing it as an indictment of the kinds of close matings that we as purebred breeders do. Even if you are in the outcross-or-die camp — an increasingly popular one these days — as a purebred dog breeder you are dealing with a closed gene pool that relies on its homozygosity to produce predictable traits of appearance and temperament.

Pomeranian

But think more deeply for a moment: In order to have the hybrid vigor that comes from crossing two different races, or breeds, or strains, you need the inbred parents. If we all become a melting pot, if we have more commonality than differences, we lose the benefit that comes from very high heterozygosity in our hybrid offspring.

In a conversation I had with a canine geneticist years ago, the subject of breeding rolled around. "I don't breed dogs, but if I did, this is the model that makes sense to me," he said, referencing the same corn scenario that Ziv discusses in his book. "I would keep two lines of dogs, and inbreed on each one independent of the other. And when I wanted a really spectacular dog, I'd cross them."

We sometimes forget that among members of a given ethnicity or nationality, there are often dramatic differences. For example, my parents are Italian. They come from an isolated mountain valley in the Dolomites, the northernmost part of the country. (Think Julie Andrews and the von Trapps making their getaway over the Alps — those are our edelweiss-dotted precincts.) My parents — and by extension, myself — have very little, if anything, in common — historically, linguistically, culinarily and certainly genetically — with someone from, say, Sicily, the island at the tip of the boot.

We have this diversity within our purebred dogs, too, especially in breeds where founding breeders developed and consolidated their bloodlines. Taking that a step further, even within one kennel, you can have a family within a family — genetically different dogs, even though they are of the same breed, even perhaps the same general bloodline. That's not very different from my parents' Alpine valley, where each town was, until recently, an island until itself, with its own families, its own variant of the dialect spoken, and — because of an intensely parochial peasant culture — its own gene pool.

The danger of talking about hybrid vigor, then, is to only see it as one rigid measure. You don't just get hybrid vigor when you cross different breeds, a la the Puggle. You also get hybrid vigor when you cross different lines within a breed, and — getting even more microcosmic — different threads within an established line.

In his book, Ziv discusses the major histiocompatability complex, or MHC, a neighborhood of genes that is involved with regulating immunity. Studies have shown that humans and animals are attracted to mates that have a different MHC than they do.

"A study of 411 Hutterite couples found that the husband and wife were more likely to have different MHCs than would be predicted by random choice," Ziv says, referring to the communal group of Anabaptists that have similar roots to the Amish, and are clustered in the Dakotas and other prairie states. "Even within this closed community, it would appear that boys and girls are subconsciously seeking out genetic diversity."

In other words, European-rooted Hutterites don't have to find a Cherokee or a Botswanan or some other member of a distant ethnic group to incorporate the diversity required for genetic well-being: They find it within their own relatively closed ethnic community. (Not to sail too glibly between human and canine examples, but this could very well explain why some bitches are dead set against breeding to a certain stud dog: They probably know something we don't. Ziv sites studies in which women were not only able to pick out men who were more symmetrical, but also those who had had high levels of MHC heterozygosity, simply by sniffing T-shirts they had slept in.)

Ziv also notes that there is a price to be paid for outcrossing. "Animals have to find a balance between the costs of inbreeding and the costs outbreeding," he writes. "They want to maximize their kids' heterozygosity so they avoid mating with close relatives. But mating with someone too different can be risky too. It's critical that the offspring be adapted to the environment where they're being born. Their survival depends on it. So mates that are too different can be a turnoff."

Bottom line: You can't have hybrids without some degree of inbreeding to precipitate them, because a hybrid needs genetically dissimilar parents. There are many conditions and states that depend on the co-existence of two opposites: good and evil, day and night, yin and tang, hot and cold, Democrat and … well, you get the idea. Five hundred years before the birth of Christ, the Greek philosopher Heraclitus came up with a name for this theory: the unity of opposites.

"The road up and the road down is one and the same," Heraclitus wrote. We're straying into metaphysics here, but basically the only certainty we have is that nothing will stay certain for long. In both our human families and our canine ones, we have condensed and diluted our gene pools constantly throughout the millennia. In one breeding, your inbred strain can produce a total outcross who is a poster child for hybrid vigor; in another, two total outcrosses who have a parent in common can create tightly inbred offspring.

Rather than fearing either extreme, perhaps we should cast a wary eye on the middle, which is something Ziv doesn't discuss in his book. But we see it eroding so many of our breeds. Thanks to matador sires and willy-nilly pairings, in many pedigrees we find no true inbreeding, nor true hybrid vigor. Instead, we have a creeping homogenization, a groupthink that is watering down many bloodlines, not unlike what is happening culturally in the human world: When gluing yourself to your iPhone, slugging down Coca-Cola, and watching reruns of "Jersey Shore" becomes your cultural norm, except you are in New Delhi, not New York, you know you're in trouble.

In our dogs and our breeding programs, we'd do well to avoid this McDonaldization, too. As for your own romantic endeavors, maybe adding "symmetrical" to your eHarmony profile wouldn't be a bad idea, either.

**Neapolitan Mastiff**, courtesy of James Deppen

# That's a Shame

*Leave your hang-ups outside the whelping box, please.*

The call came in the middle of Sussex Spaniels, and the voice on the other end of the line from Beavercreek, Ohio, held a lilt of concern.

"I see you ringside at the Garden, and it looks like you're having an argument," my friend said, as the long-bodied brown dogs circled the green carpet at Manhattan's famous Westminster dog show. "Is everything all right?"

Everything was indeed all right: Having become fluent in body language in the mild-mannered Midwest, my friend had misread the Queens accent in my flying hands and air jabs as I conversed ringside: I was being emphatic, not angry. (Although there's a lesson to us all: In this video-streaming age, no gesture or body-part adjustment goes unnoticed.)

There was, however, an impassioned discussion ensuing between myself and another friend regarding the "worthiness" of a breeding animal.

The dog in question was a typey representation of the breed, sound in both body and mind. In his first and only breeding, he had produced a serious genetic defect. It was devastating for his owner, who vowed never to breed him again. But soon after, a genetic test for the recessive gene he carried was made available, and the possibility of him being bred again was raised, as he could be bred to a clear bitch and never again produce the problem.

"Yes," my friend said, "but given what he has produced, is he really *worthy*?"

"It's not his worthiness you're talking about," I said, delivering another air jab. "It's yours."

Dog breeding is supposed to be part art, part science. Nobody ever said there had to be aspects of a dysfunctional family dinner table involved, too. It's natural to feel disappointment, or frustration, or dismay when a particular dog produces a problem. But when feelings like shame enter into the equation, then we're no longer dealing with a breeding program: We've got a people problem on our hands.

It turns out there is a name for what we dog people do when we subconsciously associate what happens in the whelping box with our sense of self-worth: It's called "projective identification."

"We all project the parts of ourselves that we want accepted onto other people and animals and objects," says psychologist, author and Bouvier fancier Dr. Joel Gavriele-Gold of Manhattan. "It's wired in — it's one of our major defenses. But it's not the healthiest defense in the world."

Fraught as it is with imperfection, dog breeding almost guarantees insecurity and self-doubt: Arm-wrestling with Mother Nature can be humbling and terrifying, sometimes at the same time. Some fanciers deal with this by leaving altogether — the famous seven-year ditch. But others cope by deflecting their fears, oftentimes on the dogs themselves.

You know them, because they exist in every breed: Smug and ever ready with the "gotcha," they troll web sites, looking for missing health screenings and offering theories about their absence. They grab at flakes of gossip like hungry goldfish, passing them on with great gusto, never bothering to verify, or asking if the person to whom they are passing it even has a need to know. They crow about the importance of open disclosure, berate those who do not do it, then use the information to fan innuendo and speculation.

Worst of all, they seed a breed culture with the wrongheaded idea that, somehow, the sins of the breeder are visited upon their dogs. This is never articulated, of course, because to simply say it aloud gives voice to how illogical it is. But the suggestion is there: That the reason bad things happen to a breeder's dogs is because somehow, somewhere, the breeder has done something to deserve it.

"If you define yourself by being in the dog-show world, then whatever happens with your dog reflects on you deeply," Gavriele-Gold points out, adding that the quest for perfection exacerbates this. We tell ourselves that there are no perfect dogs. ("I will never forget being told by an old Gundog man ... that if ever I thought I had bred the perfect dog I should immediately take it out into the field and shoot it!" wrote Catherine Sutton of Britain's well-known and large Rossut variety kennel a half-century ago.) Nonetheless, we set that as our ideal. We strive for the unattainable, though we sometimes forget to measure our progress by how close we come to it, not by how far we have fallen short.

"Mother Nature is going to do her thing, but people put it back on themselves," Gavriele-

Old English Sheepdog

Gold says. That tendency has become more commonplace as dogs are seen less as livestock, and more like family members with fur. When a human parent passes a genetic defect onto his or her child, there can be a palpable sense of shame, as if the parent is intrinsically defective or "less than."

"In terms of parenting, people say to themselves, 'What kind of parent are you that you let this happen?'" Gavriele-Gold continues.

We know that every dog carries a certain number of lethal genes; not one has escaped this reality. Sometimes, the roll of the die that is breeding brings them forward so that they express; other times, they just quietly pass to the next generation, awaiting a future turn. Just because we don't see them in a dog's phenotype doesn't mean they don't exist in the genotype. Eve was naked before she ate that famous apple; it wasn't until she was given self-awareness that she thought — wrongly, in my view — to be ashamed.

So back to our ringside discussion: It had nothing to do with "worthiness," as my old Catholic-school catechism might have defined it, about how pure our souls are or some kind of divine retribution from that great breeder in the sky. It is literally about the value of a specific dog or bitch in a specific breeding program: Is there a scenario where this dog's positive attributes benefit the breed, and what is known of the undesirable traits he produces is minimized or avoided? It is really that simple — even without a wild gesticulation for emphasis.

Ardross students with Airedales

# Maid to Order

*Looking back at a now extinct — and female dominated — profession.*

When we talk about getting an "education" in dogs, that usually means a magpie approach: snatched ringside conversations, seminars by experts both real and self-anointed, books on canine conformation with a forest of diagrams, and maybe dinner with a pillar of the breed, with the hope of a few pearls amid the *rigatoni alla vodka*.

Wasn't always so. Great Britain has a long and distinguished history of churning out master dog men and women — as well as the polished kennel help to aid them in the daily care of dozens, sometimes hundreds of dogs. The 1930s were the heyday of kennel-maid schools in the United Kingdom, a place for young ladies to learn a trade at the hands of distinguished and accomplished dog folk — many of them women themselves.

"For the real dog-lover who must earn her own living what more delightful profession can there be than that of kennel-maid?" began an article on the training program at Bell Mead Kennels in Haslemere, Surrey. "Competition, however, is keen in these advanced days, and in order to rise to the enviable heights in any sphere one must be trained."

And trained they were, in everything from feeding and grooming to exercising and whelping. Huddled around a white-coated instructor, the young women observed proper technique in bandaging injuries, brushing teeth and clipping nails. Some schools had veterinarians in on a regular basis to lecture on disease management and first aid.

Not surprisingly, many of the kennel-maid schools grew out of established breeding programs, such as the Ardross Kennelmaids College, in Ashford, Middlesex, which not only bred its line of well-known Airedales, but also incorporated the kennels of the Westrena Wire Fox and Sealyham Terriers, and Cumnoch Scottish Terriers. The Nunsoe Training Kennel for Ladies in Crawley, Sussex, had Poodles that were known around the world. Bell Mead, one of the largest English boarding kennels of the day, was famous for its Dandie Dinmont Terriers. Proximity to the great dogs of these prolific kennels gave students an opportunity to learn the intricacies of a particular breed, as well as the general care of canine boarders.

The British Pathé video archive offers several films on kennel maids, who parade everything from Saint Bernards to Salukis. In a 1931 short, the flickering silent screen shows a quote from Miss Trefusis Forbes, proprietor of Bell Mead Kennels: "The job of looking after our doggy friends is attracting more of the fair sex every year — as a business."

To be sure, kennel-maid schools provided essentially free labor for the kennels, with only the cost of room and board, and the bonus of tuition fees. Ardross noted that its numbers grew explosively in the 1930s, from two students in 1932 to a whopping 43 in 1937, with the latter class representing Australia, South Africa, Austria, Italy and Romania. In turn, the reputations of the schools — and the often titled individuals who gave their patronage, such as HRH Princess Marie Louise's affiliation with Bell Mead — meant that students were essentially guaranteed employment after graduation. "All students fitted with good posts," promised an Ardross ad.

Though the life of a kennel maid was decidedly unglamorous, tediously set to the feeding and exercise schedules of the dogs, some of the schools advertised "extras" to appeal to students.

"There is ample scope for recreation — tennis, golf, swimming, and an excellent riding school close at hand offers cheap rates to Ardross students," read an article about the kennel. "During the winter terms there are lessons in carpentering" — building kennel runs was another project assigned to kennel maids. "Continental students have the facility of combining learning or perfecting the English language with the kennel education. A certificated English teacher (B.A. of Oxford University) is on the staff, from whom they receive lessons after kennel hours."

Ardross also had a "holiday branch abroad," at Palais d'Azur, Juan Les Pins, on the French Riviera. "There is a large terrace facing the sea for sun bathing; physical culture" — what we know as yoga and isometrics — "horse riding, swimming, and for experienced swimmers, boating, surf-riding and sea-skiing," Ardross' promotional literature waxed on. "Overseas students can visit the Riviera (accompanied by one of the principals) and attend the International shows on the Continent."

Beyond the professional training and credentials they provided, kennel-maid schools offered another advantage, however unspoken: They were a haven from the gender restrictions of the day. In their androgynous uniforms — jodhpurs, shirts and ties at Bell Mead, turtlenecks and slacks at Ardross, the occasional beret in honor of the Poodle's origins at Nunsoe — the women were liberated from any preconceived gender roles. Indeed, at first glance, some of them, with their short, pageboy haircuts and lack of jewelry or makeup, could be easily mistaken for adolescent boys.

The juxtaposition of two Bell Mead film clips drives this point home. In one, a very proper-looking client comes to pick up her energetic white terrier, and is greeted by two of the kennel managers, also impeccably dressed in tailored suits, cloche hats, and nylons and dress shoes. In the other clip, 10 Bell Mead kennel maids in overalls run through a meadow toward the camera, the joyously galloping dogs barely visible in the high grass.

Just as telling is a 1934 short, titled "Greyhound Girls." Voiced over by a veddy British-sounding commentator, it rings sexist and patronizing to a modern ear, referring to women with musty biblical and mythological references: "Eve's interest in dogs and her skill in the maintenance and breeding of show specimens, from Pekingese to Poodles, has long been acknowledged and accepted as a normal happening," it begins. "But what of these Greyhound kennels, almost entirely organized and managed by fair Dianas?"

Amid footage of kennel maids soaping and bathing the racing dogs, the film notes that some 200 Greyhounds at this unidentified kennel "are kept in tip-top condition by 24 kennel maids whose occupation demands tact, patience and

Future Nunsoe Poodle champions with their kennel maids

knowledge — in fact, all those characteristics which we males thought were our own exclusive features. This is one more illusion shattered and encroaches still further on men's preserves. Well, we have to admit that she does her job more than well: Did you ever see better behaved Greyhounds?"

Just as the kennel-maid schools were beginning to come into full flower, World War II arrived. The war had a chilling effect on every strata of the dog world: The owner of Bell Mead, Dame Katherine Jane Trefusis Forbes, left the kennel in 1939 to accept a post as the first director of the Women's Auxiliary Air Force. Despite holding the rank of air commandant — equal to a brigadier in the army — she, like the kennel maids she once instructed, ran up against the gender stereotypes of the day: Only permitted to present her views and recommendations to the Air Council with a male intermediary, and constantly overruled by male colleagues, she left her military post in 1943.

Like the breeding kennels that spawned them, many of the kennel-maid schools were irrevocably shaken by the war's devastation. Though some continued on into the next half of the 20th Century, these vibrant oases of dog culture never regained the heady promise or prominence of those pre-war years. Another era, ended.

Samoyed and Australian Shepherd — no relation

# We Are Family

*A new study finds some surprising genetic connections between breeds.*

When I was a kid in the '70s, sprawled on my mother's gold shag carpet watching detective shows on the faux-wood-enshrined television, the plots followed this unwavering formula: Things happened — usually, very bad things — and wise-cracking cops solved the crimes with a combination of street smarts, sharp-elbowed confessions and a healthy pinch of luck. Their success relied heavily on intuition, a sprinkling of fingerprint powder the only high-tech flourish.

Today's Starskys and Hutches have flipped that time-tested formula: Now, hardly one episode of "Law & Order" goes by without DNA results being tossed down in front of a defiant suspect and his smarmy lawyer, who then both wilt at the prospect of a slam-dunk conviction. The message is clear: DNA does not lie. And it can wait patiently for years, or decades — or, in the case of our purebred dogs, centuries — before collaring its suspects.

In April 2017, *Cell Reports* magazine published a paper entitled "Genomic Analyses Reveal the Influence of Geographic Origin, Migration, and Hybridization on Modern Dog Breed Development." Enough words to choke an Ovcharka, but what they basically boil down to is that the DNA of various breeds — 161, to be exact — was analyzed to see how they are related. After comparing 170,000 different points on the canine genome, the scientists identified 23 "clades," or clusters, containing breeds that are significantly related.

To be sure, these researchers have a sterling pedigree: Among them is Elaine Ostrander at the National Institutes of Health, well known for her work on the Dog Genome Project, which has mapped genes responsible for body size, leg length, skull shape and fur type in dogs. But the paper didn't create many ripples in the dog press, other than a passing mention here, or a frisson of incredulity there. And that's understandable: The paper is dense and full of scientific jargon. (Allele frequencies, haplotype sharing and bootstrap cladograms, anyone?) And some of the findings are, at face value, a bit unbelievable or downright contradictory, flying in the face of some romantic myths to which we've become quite attached.

One of the biggest bombshells to come out of the paper is the idea that there was no single genetic event that created various categories of dogs. For example, the study contends, there was no ancient, mother-of-all Sighthounds whose offspring millennia later had migrated to all corners of Europe and Asia. (So, that Afghan Hound on Noah's ark? Sorry, just a story.) Instead, the DNA shows that a Sighthound type spontaneously evolved in the Mediterranean region, giving rise to Afghans, Salukis, Ibizan and Pharaoh Hounds, Azawakhs and others. At some other point in time, arbitrarily and independently, the same thing happened in the British Isles, resulting in the Greyhound, Scottish Deerhound, Irish Wolfhound and Whippet.

Not only are these two families of Sighthounds genetically distinct — which upends centuries of assumptions — but a given Sighthound has genetically more in common with the non-Sighthounds of its clade than it does with a Sighthound from outside its clade. In other words, according to the study, a Saluki is more closely related to a Great Pyrenees, which is a fellow member of the Mediterranean clade, than it is with a Greyhound, which comes from the UK Rural clade.

Similarly, the study shows that we can now bury that old chestnut about the Tibetan Mastiff being the foundation breed for all the Molossers. (For those not familiar with that word, even though the AKC once proposed a group by that name, think wrinkle and drool, though not always.) Instead, the study found, there is no genetic relationship at all: Tibetan Mastiffs cluster in a clade with Asian and Arctic spitz breeds such as Akitas and Shiba Inus. So, again, an English Mastiff is genetically closer to a Bull Terrier from its UK Rural clade than it is to those ancient temple guardians from the Tibetan plateau.

Speaking of Molossers, let's look at the Cane Corso. Its seesawing quality has a great deal to do with the various breeds introduced during its relatively recent *riconoscimento* in Italy: Literally meaning "to know again," *riconoscimento* is the process of recognition — and it often involves crossing to related or similar breeds in order to build numbers and add desired traits. It's an open secret that in Italy, Neapolitan Mastiffs and Boxers, among others, were used in the Cane Corso — and, true to form, they are reflected in the study's analysis of country-of-origin Corsos. I had a pang of "whaaaaa?" when I saw Chinook there, too — I mean, the Italians are creative, but they aren't *that* creative — but a call to the researchers explained that the Chinook result in the Cane Corso was likely an echo of the German Shepherd, a breed both the Corso and Chinook share in their backgrounds.

The Cane Corso in the United States developed somewhat independently from its mother country, which is obvious in the more substantial, "rustic" look of the old American lines. For decades, there have been unsubstantiated rumors that Neapolitan Mastiffs and Rottweilers were used on this side of the pond — resulting in, among other things, the disqualification for black-and-tan in the AKC standard, which is not specifically mentioned in its FCI counterpart. (Instead, the Italian standard makes a point of prohibiting "large white patches" — Boxer, anyone?) The genetic study found a significant difference in breed makeup between Cane Corsos in the United States and those in the country of origin. The American Corsos, it turns out, showed the strong influence of — *surprise, surprise!* — American Neapolitan Mastiffs and Rottweilers, as well as other mastiff breeds.

In terms of health issues, the study's results help explain the origins of disease-causing mutations. For example, Collie eye anomaly (CEA) affects not only Collies, but Border Collies, Shetland Sheepdogs and Australian Shepherds, which are all members of its UK Rural clade. But the disease is also present in the Nova Scotia Duck Tolling Retriever, which is in an entirely different clade. The study found the Collie and/or Shetland Sheepdog to be previously undocumented contributors to this Canadian breed, providing an explanation for how the disease traveled from one clade to another.

The same applies to the MDR1 gene mutation, which causes drug susceptibility among many British-derived herding breeds and has been found in the German Shepherd, even though it is not part of the UK Rural clade. The study posits the missing link to be the Australian Shepherd, suggesting that either that breed or a common ancestor played into the development of the modern German Shepherd Dog.

Cane Corso

Labrador Retriever

The study is chockablock with unforeseen relationships like these, which at face value raise more questions than they answer: While the study found that the Basenji was so unique that it deserved a clade all its own, its data revealed that the DNA of Basenjis outside of Africa showed an incursion of American Rat Terrier — illustrating the study's contention that a breed is altered by its migration to a new region. (Indigenous breeds are also impacted by these newcomers, which explains why native New World dogs like the Xoloitzcuintli and Peruvian Hairless Dog unexpectedly showed strong German Shepherd influence.) More food for thought: Though they are classified as Molossers elsewhere in the world, Newfoundlands were found to cluster in the same clade with retrievers. So did Dalmatians, whose origins are still so hard to pin down even the researchers aren't quite sure what to do with them. ("Might be that they're really cats," one quipped to me.)

All this goes to show that every breed is its own island — sometimes, a very inaccessible one. It's up to history-minded fanciers within each breed culture put their oars in the water to determine whether these genetic findings jibe with their breed's long-held mythology. And if the results seem irreconcilable with perceived reality, may I suggest a call to the researchers: They are accessible and willing to field questions whose answers may not be immediately discernible from the complicated charts and graphs.

Much more complicated than an episode of "NYPD Blue" — but for many purebred-dog fanciers, far more fascinating.

Saluki

# Of Highboys and Lowchen

*The Pottery Barn-ization of purebreds.*

It's been more than a decade since I visited Willie, my trusty furniture refinisher in Brooklyn.

An antiques-dealer friend made the introduction, a gesture I will always appreciate — among that highly competitive bunch, no one freely shares his sources. Willie's bustling shop in a rapidly gentrifying neighborhood just a short skip from the Brooklyn Navy Yard did restoration work for museums and high-end dealers. His men trained in the lost art of French polishing had arms like most people do thighs. And his store was filled to its tin ceilings with candelabra, rosewood étagères, marble-topped breakfronts. The inventory spilled over into the upper floors of the building next door. It was a dusty, mahogany-grained slice of heaven.

Over the years, the antiques in my home could have used a sprucing up, but I was busy navigating the white-water rapids of grade-school children, start-up businesses and, of course, the dogs, one of whom had acquired a taste for 19th Century applewood. When the tracks on the dining-room table broke — in truth, from being lifted too many times to clean the housebreaking oopses on the carpet below — I broke down and called Willie.

Turned out he was long gone from Atlantic Avenue, having moved to a decidedly untrendy neighborhood in the bowels of the borough. Along with the classical mahogany table, I was bringing him an arts-and-crafts Mission bookcase that I had bought on the street a few months earlier for $50. (Garage-sale recidivism is a terrible thing.) I started to apologize for bringing him the quarter-sawn oak piece — it wasn't high style enough for him, I knew — but he waved away my objections.

"It's work," he said.

The antiques business, it turns out, has had a reversal in fortunes. Eerily, perhaps presciently, very much like the sport of dogs.

Value is a mercurial thing, based as it is on demand. Sometimes that correlates purely to scarcity — diamonds, after all, would be costume-jewelry filler if they were as common as gravel. But public perception has much to do with it as well. The hand-carved, beautifully patinaed pieces in Willie's shop — or my living room, for that matter — are still as finely made and relatively uncommon as when they were in high demand. Nothing has changed on their end. It is the people who value them who have morphed.

The zeitgeist today is to appear as casual and unfussy as possible; it isn't chic to look studied. The tastemakers who two decades ago snapped up pink Depression-glass tumblers and Eastlake settees have become Pottery Barn and Crate & Barrel converts. The byword is convenience; no one wants to look like they worked too hard to accomplish anything, whether it's a hairstyle or a Thanksgiving spread. (Speaking of which, these days you can't *give away* vintage dinnerware or glassware sets. Rosenthal? Nippon? "No one entertains that way anymore," said Willie with a sad shake of his head.)

And so it goes with purebred dogs. The same trends, the same seismic shifts have happened here. Even discounting for a moment the social stigma that has arisen around buying instead of adopting a family companion, our dogs are seen as too fussy, too old fashioned. Instead, the whole Doodle/Puggle dynamic has eclipsed us, fueled by this idea of rejecting the tradition of the past while distilling its essence in an entirely new — and, oftentimes, frenetic — package.

Rightly or wrongly, purebred dogs are associated with elitism. Fifty years ago, it was the social norm to aspire, Don Draper like, for that big white house in the suburbs; today, nobody wants to look like they try that hard, though they still live there. You can hear it in the social commentary, as high-profile dog shows like Westminster are parodied for being beauty pageants — which, by the way, have largely fallen by the wayside in much the same way: Better the highly moussed brawls on "The Bachelor" than the measured cadences of a bathing-suit competition. And in that context, there's deep social significance to the Westminster Kennel Club adding agility to its competitive roster: It is an every-dog competition, no pedigree required.

(Ironically, the modern argument against dog-show elitism focuses on the dogs themselves, though anyone in the sport long enough knows that it was the institution itself that until not so long ago was almost exclusively the domain of wealthy WASPs.

Russell Terrier

Today our sport, and our leadership, is a healthy mix of ethnicities and religious affiliations, though people of color are still scarce, and women, though making up the majority of participants — "Where are all the men?" half-joked one judge in the midst of a hotly contested class at a national specialty recently — are woefully underrepresented in the corridors of power. But one overarching, culturally grounded problem per essay, please.)

What to do? Not much in the short term. We are off trend. I love my "old-fashioned" furniture; it's not going anywhere simply because Anthropologie has become the clarion call of the land. And I know that the pendulum swing will be coming, because such is the way of the world. When it does, my figural Victorian napkin ring holders — including an adorable *Pug*, not *Puggle*, with eerie glass eyes — will be at the ready. And in the meantime, in this fall from grace there is opportunity for those who wish to see it: Many of the pieces I longed for but couldn't afford are now in my grasp. That 19th Century Black Forest carved-bear hallstand? I'm coming for you, baby.

Similarly, breeders will continue to breed, because that's what we do, without concern about the whims and fashions of the outside world. (Though the whims and fashions of our own dog-show subculture are another story entirely.) For some breeds, this period of contraction can be a panacea, as the serious students can hunker down and correct where things have gone astray. The key is to remember the value of what we have, maintain it at all costs, and remain ready for the day when we are again the flavor of the week — with all the new problems and challenges that brings.

And if you want Willie's number, give me a call. I might just give it to you.

English Setter

# Tight Spots

*Close encounters of the breeding kind.*

You know the old saw: Those who can, do. Those who can't, teach.

Perhaps there should be an addendum, at least when it comes to dog breeding:

Those who never did, preach.

Inbreeding (or what we in dogs call linebreeding in its less intense form) is a favorite whipping boy of the critics of purebred dogs — and some within our own ranks, too. But it seems it is always the theorists — the animal rightists, the academics-steeped professors, the theriogenologically challenged veterinarians — who most vocally criticize breeders, without ever having stepped into a whelping box themselves. Would that everyone who writes an article, films a documentary or posts on Facebook about how breeders should breed be required to plan, whelp, rear and follow a dozen litters — not just one or two, as that does not give the breeding gods adequate time to deliver their cruel curveballs.

Indeed, rarely is it the long-term and successful breeder (the two adjectives are not mutually inclusive) who gets on the bully pulpit about the perils of linebreeding. The more accomplished the breeder, the fewer absolutes he or she dispenses. That's because being in the trenches has a way of humbling you. The theoretical gives way to Mother Nature, who is as ruthless and stealthy in getting her way as a subway pickpocket.

All this isn't to say that linebreeding won't reveal deleterious genes: It can, and will. In the short term, that is a blow to everyone — the owner, the breeder and not least of all the affected dog. But the alternative — outcrossing to avoid doubling up on common ancestors — can have an even more devastating, albeit delayed outcome, as the problematic gene goes undetected and seeds itself in the breed population, creating a morass for unsuspecting breeders several generations down the line. There is no shame in uncovering or producing a genetic problem in a breed — only in not dealing with it when it arises.

And the truth is, any act of procreation — whether of a protozoa or a Pomeranian — leaves the door ajar to peril. We humans "breed" and produce genetic defects all the time. Genes recombine, recessives line up, mutations emerge. Breeders are just more acutely aware of the hazards of embarking on a new generation because we are proactively engineering these pairings, noting their outcomes, and immortalizing them in our pedigrees.

Inbreeding is simply a tool. Like a hammer or a chainsaw, it can be used deftly, or with calamitous results. Geneticists like Jerold Bell, DVM (himself a Gordon Setter breeder), have shown that having islands of linebred families — all of which are linebreeding on *different dogs*, a key point — maintains as much genetic diversity in a given breed as constant outcrosses.

Linebreeding is a system routinely employed in other domesticated species, from pigeons to pigs. (Years ago while working on a newspaper story, I visited a crusty breeder of homing pigeons in his grotto-like garage under an underpass in Queens; he had to linebreed, he told me, pointing to his most recent downy-feathered clutch, to get and keep the correct length of wing feathers to give his birds endurance and speed for those long-distance flights.) But the use of linebreeding in dogs is clouded by our insistent anthropomorphism: The more we as a culture consider dogs to be human surrogates, the more uncomfortable we are made by "incestuous" pairings that are taboo in most modern societies. (And ancient ones, too: Oedipus, anyone?)

This taboo likely arose from pragmatic reasons as much as moral ones: Some species are just more tolerant of inbreeding than others (the same is true of individuals or lines within a given species or breed), and humans aren't one of them. When we "double up," disaster often befalls. Charles Darwin, the father of evolutionary biology, was steadfastly against "consanguinity" — literally, "blood relation" — because he saw the direct effects of it in his own family: He and wife Emma Wedgwood (yes, those Wedgwoods of porcelain fame) were first cousins, and Darwin's mother, Susannah Wedgwood, was the daughter of third cousins. Of the Darwins' 10 children, three died at early ages and three were never able to have children of their own. Inbreeding depression? No way to say for sure, but it sounds like it.

"The consequences of close inbreeding carried on for too long a time are, as is generally believed, loss of size, constitutional vigor and fertility, sometimes accompanied by a tendency to malformation," Darwin wrote in 1878. "That any evil directly follows from the closest interbreeding has been denied by many persons, but rarely by any practical breeder and never, as far as I know, by one who has largely bred animals which propagate their kind quickly."

But four decades after Darwin's death, an American biologist named Helen Dean King challenged those strongly held beliefs about close breeding — with a world-famous strain of albino laboratory rats.

A brilliant woman in a decidedly man's world, King was a Vassar and Bryn Mawr graduate whose work at the Wistar Institute of Anatomy and Biology in Philadelphia in the early 1900s led to the development of the "Wistar rat." Characterized by its wide head and long ears, this heavily inbred white rat soon was in great demand for laboratory research all over the world — and today about half of the world's lab rats are descend from this Philly-raised family. The rats all came from a colony King bred, in brother to sister pairings — the closest form of inbreeding possible — over and over, for some 30 generations.

Local newspapers had a field day with King's not-so-mousy demeanor: "Women Afraid of Rats? Here's One Who Raises 'Em" dished a 1922 headline on a profile of King in the Philadelphia *Evening Public Ledger*. But King's research, spanning some 40 years, was as meticulous as it was groundbreaking.

In her 1918 book *Studies on Inbreeding*, King wasted no time in evoking Darwin to illustrate what she called "the almost universal prejudice against inbreeding" — he is quoted on the book's very first page. King pointed out that many wild-animal species do perfectly well in small, isolated communities with a high level of inbreeding. But in her austere lab, it looked like Darwin's doom-mongering was on target: As King detailed how she started her inbred rat line — using four rats to create two parallel lines — she described what sounded like a classic case of inbreeding depression.

Chinese Shar-Pei

"In the earlier generations the inbred rats exhibited all of the defects which are popularly supposed to appear in any closely inbred stock," she wrote. "Many females in both series were sterile, and those that did breed usually produced only one or two litters which were generally of small size. A considerable proportion of the rats were dwarfed, or stunted in their growth, and many of them developed malformations, particularly deformed teeth." The rats also showed "a steady decline in vitality in succeeding generations, and usually died at a relatively early age."

Had King discontinued the experiments at that point, Darwin's opinion would have been upheld. But King observed that many of the other rats in her general colony, which were *not* inbred, were showing the same characteristics.

Something other than genetics was to blame, she surmised, and she soon discovered what it was.

"The rats were fed chiefly on bread soaked in milk and on corn; meat and vegetables were given only once a week," she wrote. A "radical" change was made to the rats' unbalanced feeding regimen that better reflected their scavenger nature: "Milk and fresh bread were eliminated from the diet, and 'scrap' food, consisting of carefully sorted table refuse, was fed once each day."

After the improved nutrition, the change in the rats was startling. "The animals gained in size and in weight, sterility almost disappeared, and the average number of young in the litters was increased," King wrote. The problem with malformed teeth also virtually vanished. And so, with a simple change of diet, King remediated the "dire effects of inbreeding," which did not reappear even after she bred 28 more generations of brother-to-sister crosses.

With an emphasis on selective inbreeding, King chose only the most vigorous, largest offspring to produce the next generation of Wistar rats. As a result, later generations of the rats were heavier than earlier ones, despite being more inbred. King theorized "the use of only the most vigorous animals for breeding purposes has seemingly overcome any tendency that inbreeding might have to shorten the life of the individuals." The inbred rats of later generations grew into slightly heavier adults than the non-inbred rats King used as controls.

Because of her interest in sex determination, King also made some breeding decisions based on gender ratios in the rat litters. In her A line — what she called her "male line" — she only bred from litters that contained an excess of males; conversely, in her B line, or "female line," she discarded any litters that did not have a large number of females. Her results showed that sex ratio of offspring was genetically influenced to some degree, though other factors also came into play — including season of the year and age of the mother.

Turning away from her rarified white rodents, King also studied the effects of domestication by breeding 25 generations of wild gray Norway rats; her six foundation breeding pairs were trapped in the Philadelphia streets. In addition to noting that later generations grew more quickly and much larger than their wild forbearers, King theorized that domestication contributed to an increase in genetic mutations: When the breeding was controlled by humans and not the vagaries of nature, older animals were permitted to breed, at an age where their genome was arguably less stable and more susceptible to mutations.

Like many of her colleagues in the study of genetics in the 1920s and '30s, King embraced the eugenics movement — the belief that some people are genetically superior to others, and that breeding for "super humans" is possible and even desirable. We all know where this unfortunate line of thinking led us in 1930s and '40s Germany. However, "a rat is *not* a pig is a dog is a boy," to paraphrase that quote from PETA founder Ingrid Newkirk, and one need not advocate genetic "purity" in humans to appreciate the solid science King left behind for animal breeders.

The misconceptions of her generation aside, King's work with *Rattus norvegicus* has dramatic implications for those of us tooling around in *Canis familiaris* gene pools: It offers the promise that we can create healthy, fertile families of closely related dogs with selective inbreeding — emphasis on the word "selective." It demonstrates the importance of environment — the "nurture" part of the nature-versus-nurture equation — in particular that of a biologically appropriate diet. It explains patterns that breeders note in the dogs, including the fact that some bitches tend to "throw" a preponderance of either males or females, in defiance of the law of averages.

And perhaps most important, it reminds that those in the trenches — those doing the breedings, meticulously logging the results, and selecting the most sound, vigorous and fertile stock to go forward — are those best suited to pass judgment on the vices and virtues of any breeding system.

German Shepherd Dog

Staffordshire Bull Terrier

# What's In a Name?

*When it comes to breed shorthand, more than you might think.*

Standing ringside, the three American English Coonhounds could have been an apparition, so rare is their presence at an all-breed show.

I approached their breeder-handler and asked if I could meet up with her later to discuss and go over her dogs. She graciously agreed. But as I walked away, a Coonhound friend caught me gently by the elbow.

"Don't call them American English Coonhounds," she said. "Just say you want to talk about her English dogs."

As I discovered at that moment, American English Coonhound fanciers do not refer to their dogs as American English Coonhounds, and to do so telegraphs a lack of familiarity with their breed. They are, quite simply, "English dogs."

Most other AKC-recognized breeds don't quibble about their official names — or not anymore, at least: In the 1920s and '30s, many Russian Wolfhound fanciers rejected the "Borzoi" moniker, with breed authority Louis Murr writing that "any sane breeder can see why the name Russian wolfhound should be retained." He lost that battle in 1936, when Borzoi became official.

Why should fanciers get so exorcised over simple semantics? Because words have power, and what we choose to call ourselves — or, more to the point, what we allow others to call us — reflects our identity.

Today we can see this most clearly in the shorthand names that we use for our breeds. In most cases, there is a "right" way to shorten a breed name, and a wrong way. And if you come from outside the breed, that might not seem so obvious.

In my own breed, for example, the accepted shorthand is Ridgeback. Not "Rhodesian" — or, God forbid, "Rhodie." No one has ever to my knowledge articulated why this is so, but I would bet the mortgage that it comes down to breed identity. What makes the Rhodesian Ridgeback unique is not that it comes from Rhodesia (which is Zimbabwe now anyway, and, besides, South Africa made just as significant a contribution to the breed). No, what makes a Rhodesian Ridgeback special is the ridge on its back. This is also why the breed name was changed early on from African Lion Dog: While any dog can hunt lion (although perhaps not as successfully), not every dog can have a ridge. Someone might want to tell that to the FCI, which is now seriously contemplating a ridgeless variety.

When it comes to nicknames, many other breeds also clip off their geographic identifiers in order to amplify breed purpose. Irish Wolfhounds are called Wolfhounds not just because there are lots of other Irish breeds, but because they originally hunted wolves — so well, in fact, that they led to the species' extinction and then, eventually, their own, until Captain Graham showed up.

An exception that proves this rule is the Siberian Husky. They are Siberians, not Huskies, thank you very much, and for reasons that again trace back to function. "'Husky' has a connotation of bulk and heaviness, and that's absolutely what we do *not* want in our dogs," explains breeder-judge Cindy Stansell.

(In the 1990s, the Siberian Husky Club of America contemplated a name change to the Chukchi Indian Dog, in honor of the native peoples who developed the breed, but ultimately opted not to, blessedly avoiding the specter of the uninitiated referring to the "Chuck E. Cheese Dog." Shades of the ice-creamy *spumoni* references that Spinone Italiano fanciers must contend with ...)

Many fanciers bristle at cutesy abbreviations, along the lines of the aforementioned "Rhodie." "I say Sibe, but I'm chastised for it," chuckles Stansell's husband, Robin. Similarly, "Dobie" is rejected by Doberman Pinscher folk. "This is a noble breed," says long-time fancier Vicki Seiler-Cushman. "It's a Doberman ... *not* a Dobie."

In some cases, a breed's tenure in the American Kennel Club pantheon contributes to its claim to a nickname. Going back to Irish breeds, the Irish Water Spaniel is referred to colloquially as the Water Spaniel, seemingly disregarding the existence of the American Water Spaniel. But the Irish Water Spaniel has always been in the AKC's orbit as one of the nine breeds originally recognized by the registry in 1877. And so, both historically and semantically, it got there first.

As for the American Water Spaniel, in Sporting circles it's simply called the American.

Just when you attempt to see a pattern in all this shortening of breed names, there is the inevitable curveball. Consider the Afghan Hound. That's it: Afghan Hound. Don't shorten it, fanciers warn: An Afghan is a person, while an Afghan Hound is a dog.

That point was brought home at the start of the war in Afghanistan, when anti-Saddam sentiment was at its peak. One fancier whose vanity plate read "AFGHANS" received a new one from her state department of motor vehicles. Another who had a bumper sticker that read "On the Seventh Day God Created Afghans" earned hostile gestures from nearby drivers. And in 2001, the Afghan Club of America briefly contemplated a name change to something less geographically identifiable, like Tazi.

As for the English dogs who ignited the idea for this article, nowhere else is the breed referred to as an American English Coonhound except in the American Kennel Club. (It's the English Coonhound in the UKC.) But the name of the parent club, the American English Coonhound Club, appears to have given risen to the moniker. "Had the club been called the English Coonhound Association of America …" another Coonhound aficionado mused to me.

But no matter what the reason for the verbal gymnastics, now they're just plain old English dogs to me.

Icelandic Sheepdog

Doberman Pinscher

# A Dog-Show Fairy Tale

*Move over, Sleeping Beauty.*

Once upon a time, there was a new judge named Florian* who had his first big assignment in a land far, far away.

Arriving at the dog show bright and early, Florian checked in with his fairy godmother.

(* Though Florian is the official name given to Snow White's animated prince — and Prince Charming of Sleeping Beauty fame reportedly goes by Henry — no identification with magical persons real or imagined is intended nor should be inferred.)

Florian knew that it was the job of fairy godmothers to materialize at ringside, with or without a burst of glitter, to watch new judges and make sure they were making intelligent choices, unencumbered by malevolent spells or confounding elixirs. Wand in hand, the fairy godmother scanned the list of breeds that fair Florian was to judge. After some consideration, she determined that today, at least, more would not be more.

"I won't be watching you," the fairy godmother said to Florian, holstering her wand, which shot out a feeble spray of sparks in protest.

Florian was elated at the prospect of finally letting his guard down. No notes to take, no decisions to defend, no dreaded check boxes — "Further study recommended" — to fend off.

"No one is watching," he thought to himself. "What a relief." Thus unencumbered, he went forth to slay his dragons — metaphorically speaking, of course.

The day progressed beautifully. Florian did a bang-up job in Babylonian Basilisks. The previous night's review of the Serpentine Celtic Shepherd illustrated standard proved to have been time well spent, as his judging of that breed went off without a hitch. And gauging from the ringside applause at Elysian Unicorn Hounds, he had nailed that, too.

Then he arrived at his final breed of the day, Macedonian Mastiffs.

Florian had a good grounding in Macedonians; his aunt had bred them and even had one go Best in Show a few centuries earlier. There was a lovely entry of class dogs — a major, actually — and Florian found an easy winner from the puppy class who had all the hallmarks of the breed, from the tip of his trifurcated nose to the stub of his bludgeon tail.

Then in walked the lone class bitch.

The wizard at the end of her leash was doing a masterful job presenting his charge, but it was painfully obvious to Florian that this was a pet-quality Macedonian Mastiff.

Florian heard his aunt's raspy voice in his ear. "I would not feed that."

Florian knew he was within his rights to withhold the first-place and winners ribbons, but he awarded them anyway, keenly aware that the bitch had not earned any points. Yet.

As the steward called out the numbers for the Best of Breed competition, a line of typey, sound Macedonian Mastiff champions entered the ring. Bringing up the rear were Florian's handsome Winners Dog — and his dubious Winners Bitch.

Florian examined, gaited and mentally sorted the entry, easily settling on which would be his Best of Breed, Best of Opposite, and the two Selects. But what to do about Best of Winners?

Florian looked again at the Winners Bitch, whose handler was frantically baiting her with a piece of smoked sphinx in a futile effort to give her a neck. If he awarded her Best of Winners, she too would earn the same number of championship points as the Winners Dog. That would make the handler happy, and who doesn't like a happy handler? No one would care. No one would even know.

"After all, no one is watching," Florian reminded himself.

He pulled out his Best of Breed dog. Surveying the lineup again, Florian was just about to gesture to the Winners Bitch when something welled up inside him. It wasn't that morning's porridge, though that's a good guess. No, it was his integrity.

Florian pointed to the dog for Best of Winners, and the bitch left the ring without a point, much less the coveted major, which, if you know Macedonian Mastiffs, is getting harder and harder to come by these days.

His judging complete, Florian turned his book into the superintendent, got his tear sheets and catalog, and sought out his fairy godmother to say goodbye before undertaking the long carriage ride home.

He found her in the hospitality tent, dipping a phoenix feather in her inkwell as she filled out yet-another evaluation form.

"I was ringside at Macedonian Mastiffs today," the fairy godmother announced, dusting the glitter off the chair beside her, and motioning him to sit.

Florian nearly collapsed at the thought of what he had almost done, but instead just nodded brightly.

"I was standing with a group of Macedonian breeders," the fairy godmother continued. "And they all said to me, 'He's going to cross the major over. He's going to give it to that terrible example of a Macedonian Mastiff.'

"And I said, 'I don't think so,'" the fairy godmother replied. "'Wait and see.'"

On the long ride home, Florian pondered just how closely he had come to wrecking his reputation with not just his fairy godmother, whose opinion meant a great deal to him, but the entire Macedonian Mastiff community. He winced at his internal debate, at how he almost let himself take the path of least resistance, even though he knew it was wrong.

And as the thatched roof of his home came into view, with that comforting squiggle of smoke wafting from the chimney, Florian promised himself he would never forget the obvious moral of this story:

Someone is always watching.

Remember that, and you are assured to live — and judge — happily ever after.

Bulldog

Dog gallery at Tring

# Mounting Concern

*Stuffed lions and tigers and dogs, oh, my.*

I've learned through hard experience that there are basically two reactions to the mention of taxidermied dogs: One is "That's disgusting." The other is "That's fascinating." If you count yourself among the former, you'd be advised to stop reading now.

As Britain's — and the world's — biggest dog show, Crufts is of course all about canines *with* pulses. But on my first visit to this bucket-list show ("A Crufts virgin!" exclaimed friends when I saw them on the other side of the pond), my three traveling companions and I set aside a day to view a collection of taxidermied purebred dogs improbably nestled in the Hertfordshire countryside.

The onomatopoeically named village of Tring — can you hear an old rotary-phone chirpily *b-ringgging* when you say it aloud? — is about an hour and a half southeast of the bustling show held at National Exhibition Centre in Birmingham. As Toy dogs were streaming toward the NEC's cavernous exhibition halls, we were motoring along British byways, struggling to override the urge to veer into the right lane and craning our necks to glimpse newborn lambs in the fields.

Our destination, the Natural History Museum at Tring, was once the private museum of Lionel Walter Rothschild — yes, *those* Rothschilds. As eccentric as he was disinterested in the family banking business, the budding baron declared at the tender age of seven that he would grow up to "make a museum." It was no idle threat: Within a couple of years he had amassed an impressive collection of beetles, butterflies, birds, fish and mammals. A mob of kangaroos hopped languidly around the estate grounds, and later

Rothschild's zebra-pulled wagon

Rothschild famously had a stable of zebras that he put in harness to draw his carriage, also crossbreeding them with horses to produce hybrids called zebroids.

When Rothschild turned 21, his parents gifted him with the funding and land for his longed-for museum, and a handful of years later, in 1892, he opened the doors to what became the largest zoological collection ever assembled by one person.

At the time, a Victorian visitor to the charming brick building marveled at its contents, from "a bulky Indian sawfish of unpardonable length" to a "big brute" of a white rhinoceros. At its peak, Rothschild's collection included 300,000 bird skins, 200,000 bird eggs, 2,250,000 butterflies and 30,000 beetles, as well as thousands of mammals, reptiles and fish.

But no dogs.

Having no connection to Rothschild but for their residence in his museum, Tring's collection of 88 taxidermied dogs was assembled piecemeal at the Natural History Museum in London. After World War II, the preserved canines were sent to Tring, where they reside in its furthest corner and final gallery, number six, across from towering glass display cases of snakes and amphibians.

I suppose floor-to-ceiling cases of stuffed purebred dogs *are* a bit macabre. (At least that's what the Facebook comments revealed when we posted selfies taken in front of motionless Mastiffs and stationery Salukis.) But for serious students of purebred dogs, any ick factor is soon overtaken by awe for what lessons these frozen-in-time dogs have to teach us, particularly in terms of how much some of them have evolved in the intervening century.

Consider, for example, the smooth Dachshund on display, a prizewinner bred in 1906 who is easily double the size of contemporary dogs today — even more striking when you realize she was a bitch. Lady of the Valley, the sign told us, showed the "typical build" of the breed a hundred years ago: heavier head, longer legs and narrower chest. There is no doubt in my mind that she could have taken on a badger — and won.

Another eye-opener was a pair of Bull Terriers, an unnamed white male donated in 1933 and a brindle-and-white male presented a year later. Positioned so their head profiles were clearly visible, neither dog had the distinctive egg-shaped head for which the breed is known today. But one could easily see the filled-in stops, and almond-shaped eyes, that are harbingers of what is to come. And that applied, too, to the nearby Toy Bull Terrier, a relatively delicate breed that eventually morphed into the mini-Bull Terrier.

Some of the dogs were practically unidentifiable without a quick glance at the exhibit label: Champion Hadley Hurtle, a winner of 20 championships bred in 1914, was so long on leg and short of coat as to be indistinguishable as a Sealyham Terrier. But others gave a glimpse into

Dachshund

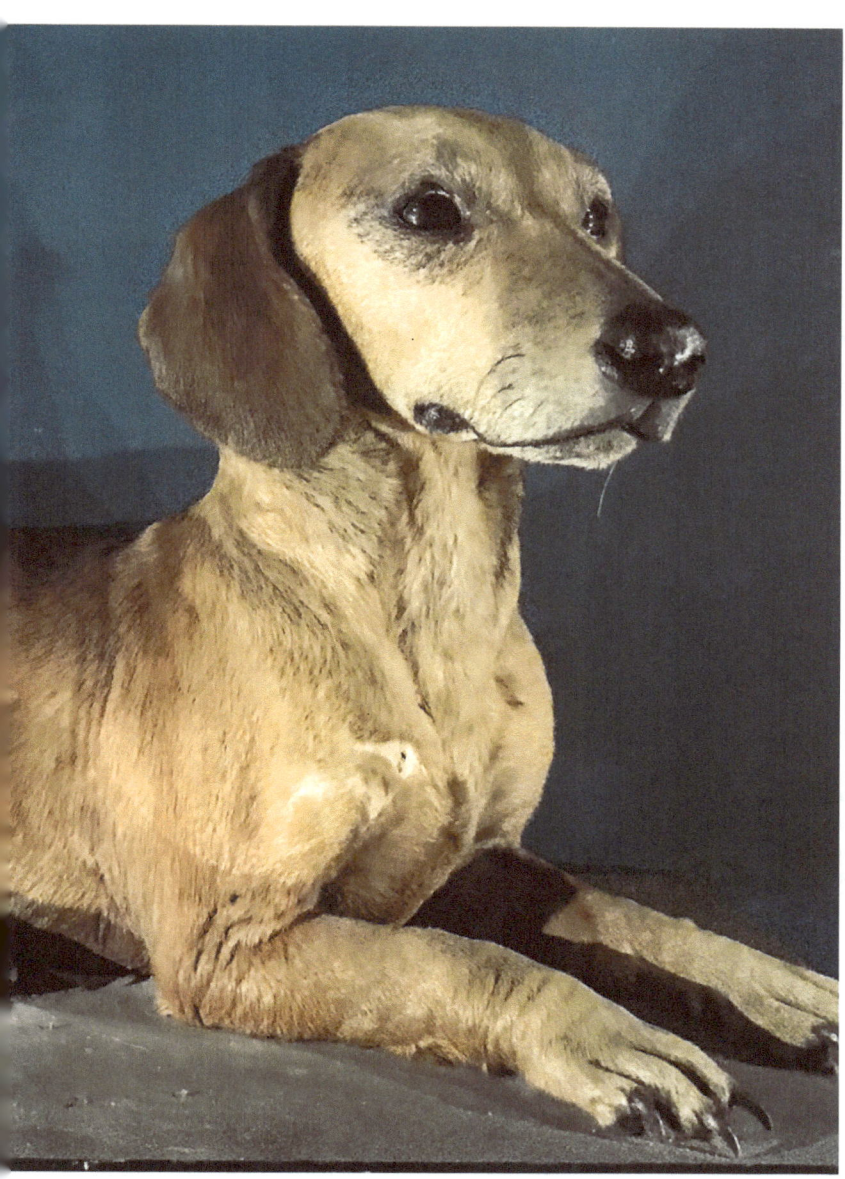

the mixing and melding that helped develop our modern dogs: The brindle Mastiff dating from the early 20th Century had only the slightest undulation of wrinkle on his head, and his relatively lithe body suggested a possible contribution from the likes of the houndy Great Dane standing beside him.

Not surprisingly, some important foundation dogs can be found at Tring, including Ah Cum, a male Pekingese imported from China in 1896 who sired many of England's early champions — and who, with his length of leg and minimal coat, at first might be mistaken for a Tibetan Spaniel. (As for the two Tibbies on display, their snipey muzzles were a world

**Sealyham Terrier**

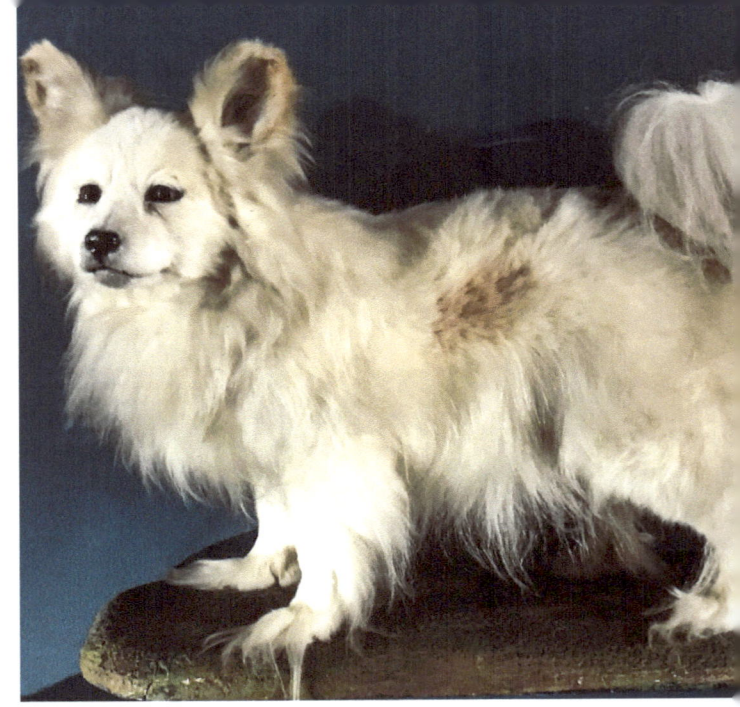

**Papillon**

**Cavalier King Charles Spaniel**

**Bull Terrier**

away from modern head type.)

Perhaps most significant among the Asiatic dogs was Tajan, a male Chinese happa dog whelped in 1906. This ancient breed was likely the rootstock for the Pekingese and perhaps also the Pug. Tajan's relatively extreme, brachycephalic head type begged the question — to me, at least — of whether the refinement of purebred dogs in the last century is less a question of extremity and more one of maturity. After all, the Chinese

Dogue de Bordeaux

had almost three millennia to perfect the happa dog, and Peking-procured Tajan looked more like a modern purebred than the majority of the Western-bred dogs displayed at Tring.

Back to family trees: When I came across a Brussels Griffon named Partridge Hill Posy, I emailed the photograph to respected breeder and judge Jeff Bazell, who, as I expected, knew her well. "I went to Tring many years ago and guess who was at the 'grooming parlor,' as they called it, for a cleaning and restoration … Posy!" he wrote back. "She is actually behind some of our dogs, as her grandsire was a black-and-tan English Toy Spaniel and she is thereby behind every black and tan Griffon. Her daughter, Partridge Hill Pollynaise, was the first black-and-tan champion in the breed."

Tring is home to a handful of modern dogs, too. One is Spike, a Victorian Bulldog whelped in 1992. Despite its name, the Victorian Bulldog is a modern breed, created by the late Kenneth Mollett to approximate a more active Bulldog type, abetted with the addition of Bull Terrier, Staffordshire Terrier and Bullmastiff blood.

Another relative newcomer is Ballyregan Bob, whelped in 1983, who is considered one of the greatest Greyhounds to have raced in Great Britain. He won 41 of his 47 races, breaking 15 track speed records along the way. We spent a good while comparing him to Fullerton, a much more moderately constructed but just as successful brindle who coursed in Britain a hundred years before.

Tring's oldest dog exhibits are also among its most fascinating: Displayed alongside a Papillon that dwarfs them were a Mexican lap dog from 1843 and a Russian lap dog from 1861. Both were white and fluffy and positively Lilliputian; either could have taken up residence in a guinea-pig cage. A decade after the Mexican dog was donated, the Rev. John George Wood was similarly impressed when he saw it at the British Museum. "If it were not in so dignified a locality, it would be generally classed with the mermaid, the flying serpent and the Tartar lamb as an admirable example of clever workmanship," he wrote in *The Illustrated Natural History (Mammalia)* in 1853. And his too-good-to-be-true radar was spot on: Both dogs are very likely youngsters, as any adult of that size would have soon succumbed to chronic hypoglycemia, the fate of most "teacups," no matter what the breed.

Their size aside, there's another thing that separated these mini-me lapdogs from the vast majority of the other canines at Tring: They no longer exist, and in that respect they resonate in only an arms-length way. Because they reflect our times, and in many respects ourselves, dog breeds must evolve. Otherwise, they are doomed to extinction, like the Bullenbeisser, or Paisley Terrier, or Tweed Water Spaniel ... the list goes on and on.

Human beings, after all, are hard-wired to experiment, create, dabble, evolve. Remember that Woody Allen line? A relationship is like a shark, his character Alvy Singer explained in "Annie Hall": "It has to constantly move forward or it dies. And I think what we got on our hands is a dead shark."

Happily, most of the dog breeds at Tring have managed to tread water with us throughout the decades, centuries, in some cases even millennia. We have survived and evolved together, even as the emphasis has largely shifted from working ability to companionship. Rather than mourning the gulf between where a given breed started — and who gets to pick exactly where on the continuum that is? — and where it has landed today, we should celebrate the fact that, thanks to the dedication of their breeders, most are still with us in *any* form. Far better to have them thronging to the green carpets of the National Exhibition Centre in Birmingham than inside the still, somber glass cases of a funny little museum in the Hertfordshire countryside.

## MORE BOOKS BY REVODANA PUBLISHING

**Little Kids and Their Big Dogs:** Volumes 1, 2 and 3

**The Afghan Hound:** Interviews with the Breed Pioneers

**The Art of the French Bulldog**

**The Best of Babbie:** The Wicked Wisdom of Babbie Tongren, the Afghan Hound's Sharpest Wit

**Everyone's Guide to the Bullmastiff**

**The Leonberger:** A Comprehensive Guide to the Lion King of Breeds

**The Official Book of the Neapolitan Mastiff**

**Your Rhodesian Ridgeback Puppy:** The Ultimate Guide to Finding, Rearing and Appreciating the Best Companion Dog in the World

**Exploring the Tibetan Mastiff:** A Love Letter in Photographs

**The Canadian Inuit Dog:** Icon of Canada's North

## ESPECIALLY FOR CHILDREN

**Peyton Goes to the Dog Show**

**How the Rhodesian Ridgeback Got Its Ridge**

www.revodanapublishing.com

www.ingramcontent.com/pod-product-compliance
Lightning Source LLC
Chambersburg PA
CBHW050753110526
44592CB00003B/53